The Beauty of Summer

The beauty of summer

BY

CANON SHEEHAN

THE MERCIER PRESS

CORK and DUBLIN

THE MERCIER PRESS, 4 Bridge Street, Cork
25 Lower Abbey Street, Dublin 1

This edition 1973

SBN 85342 328 8

PUBLISHERS NOTE

This is a reprint of part of Canon Sheehan's famous book *Under the Cedars and the Stars*. The remaining parts are published under the following titles:

The Sadness of Autumn

The Loneliness of Winter

The Magic of Spring

CONTENTS

SECTION I.

SECTION II.

SECTION III.

SECTION I.

The sense of Beauty

What a curious thing is our sense of beauty and proportion! How far we take it, and then tire of it! The ambition of every amateur gardener is to imitate in his flower-beds tapestries or wall-papers – what is technically known as carpet-gardening. Few attain to its perfection, which generally consists in an outer rim or embankment of grey garden leeks, with their pretty blossoms, which are ruthlessly stripped off because they spoil the proportion of colours; an inner border of blue or white lobelia, with its delicate medicinal blossoms; then a deep purple circle of beet-root, within which are ranged row after row of geraniums of all forms and colours, until the centre oriflamme of yellow or deep bronzed calceolarias is finally reached. The compactness, leaving no space of brown earth visible, the evenness, which will allow no blossom to spring beyond the common level; the gradations of colour, contrasting with the emerald of the closely cropped sward all around are the elements and constituents of the beauty achieved with infinite pain and care. Then, suddenly your eye rests on a page from Florence or Rome, contemptuously decrying this well ordered and prim perfection in contrast with the tropical luxuriance of Italy run wild; and lo! you accept the verdict, and turn away from your English garden, and pine for a wild flower in the forest, or the coloured mosses by some mountain stream.

9

Reversion to Nature

It is the eternal protest of Nature against its great rival, Art; and somehow the untamed heart of man responds to it. It is a tradition, probably well founded, that a savage who has been reclaimed even in infancy, clothed, fed, educated in the lap of civilization, will, if ever he get the chance of going back to his tribe, fling aside the trappings of civilized life, and taking up his blanket, revert to the primitive condition of savagery again. And no doubt, Nature itself, instead of moving onwards to artificial perfection according to the theory of the evolutionist, is ever seeking to get back to its savage state. Let the hand of man be taken from her for a moment, and back she goes to prairies, and 'forests primeval,' and tangled bushwoods, and takes once more her savage clubs to her breast. And is there not something half-akin to this in our own yearnings to leave behind the prim, Quaker-like perfection of the lawn and the garden, and the trim drawing-room with all its pretty appurtenances, and spend one day at least on the breast of Mother Nature in all her savage solitude, her mosses our couch, her forest trees our canopy, her streams and seas our music, and her vast silence our medicine to nerves and brain fretted by all the noises and artificialities of life?

The pathos of cities

The pathos of great cities is overwhelming. The submerged, shuffling along the pavements, side by side, with their brothers and sisters who float just now with the tide, but some of whom are certainly destined to be themselves submerged; the anxiety of the young to attain to position and wealth; the anxiety of the middle-aged to retain these slippery treasures; the loungers in the park not knowing well how to kill time; the ministers to human vanity in the shops; the stricken ones, wearily plodding along with mothers or sisters to seek help in the back, dark parlour of some noted physician; the many colossal and forbidding mansions of disease, or sin, or death; the alarm bell of the ambulance with its horrible freight of wrecked or broken humanity; the Courts of Justice and condemned cells; and, perhaps, worst of all, the stately gas-lit apartments, where men and women, in despair of happiness, seek its meretricious rival, excitement – all is melancholy and overpowering. It is the aggregate of misery that strikes you. In the country unhappiness is fairly divided. Here and there a mortal fretting under his load and seeking relief. But he is only a speck against the azure. In cities, unhappiness seems a cloud that blots out heaven altogether.

The evergreen

But, somehow, one of the most pathetic things in a great city is the aspect of an evergreen shrub which planted within a black iron railing just outside some fashionable drawing-room window seeks to wear out its wretched life in that prison. Just above it, perhaps, in a square decorated box are hyacinths in spring, or white begonias in summer; and every morning, some fair jewelled hand or perhaps the white, pure finger of a child is stretched out shyly to give them the little water that keeps up their artificial life. No face bends over them. That is as much against our conventionalities, as if every house was a harem. But no one heeds that poor shrub. With dry sapless roots, tainted and blackened leaves, it looks wearily at the sun, until, as in a kind of leprosy, leaves droop, and wither, and fall down; then the wrinkled little branches become dry sticks; and one day it is seen that only a blackened skeleton remains. It has pined for its forest-life, for winds and rains, for the soft burden of the snow; for the pleasant, but hurried visit of the blackbird or thrush, perhaps for the soft nest where the young of both are laid. It is an exile in this wilderness of brick. It eats out its heart and – dies.

Summer Twilights

The most lonely thing in cities is a summer twilight. Summer twilights, however beautiful, are supremely melancholy. The vesperal song of birds, the swift groupings of swallows overhead, the return of the rooks in stately procession, the steely blueness or purple of eastern skies, the branched trees, black against the daffodil sky, where the sunlight yet lingers, the swift whirr of the bats, the dancing of the midges, the closing of the flowers, are all harbingers of night; and as yet we deem night as a kind of death, until we know better. It is all very sweet, and tender, and beautiful, but there is a note of sadness somewhere. Hence, I have heard many say, that in these beautiful twilights, which, with us, stretch up to ten o'clock and further, they yearn for the cosy fireside of winter, and the companionship of blazing logs, and the book, and the music and the tea-urn. It is quite clear that this feeling is begotten of the common natural impulse to regret the end, or the departure, or the close of anything that has become familiar to us. It is the sadness of all 'Farewells' – at the railway station, at the pier, at the door, at the marriage service, and most of all at the grave, especially, when those without faith, say the final fare-well, as poor Huxley over his dead child. It is less poignant with us, who, as in Swiss cemeteries, always write on the tombstone, *Auf Wiedersehen.*

The mysterious night

This must have been what the Psalmist had in his mind when he said or sang: 'In the evening weeping shall have place; and in the morning, gladness.' For, in the morning, we come out of the far land of dreams and mystery and emerge into the glad realities of life. In the evening, the realities begin to fade all around us, and we are about to enter into the unknown and trackless ways of sleep and oblivion. There is a certain reluctance in all human hearts to venture on the mysterious or unexperienced. We cling to what we know. We dread the unrevealed. Children invariably hate to be taken away from the company of the living, and to be left with the companionship of the dark. All day long they played in the sunshine. Now shadows impenetrable gather around them. They are alone – and alone with the impalpable and mysterious. And they dread it. The feeling is shared even by grown-up people. The mysteries of night, however

13

beautiful, are mysteries, and we pine for the visible and the real. Hence, too, is prayer more suitable for the evening than for the morning. The swift delight of coming out of the shadowy land into the sunshine does not dispose to prayer. But at night, we move into the shadows again; and the awe and reverence that are all around us, penetrate our souls. We kneel and think and become reverent. And then we pray.

And Death

How did Blanco White come to write his famous sonnet, 'To Night,' (probably the only instance in literature where Fame has been summoned by one poem in fourteen lines) if he had then abandoned his faith? His comparison of Night and Death is a purely Catholic idea. The natural trembling of humanity for

> This lovely frame,
> This glorious canopy of light and blue,

is what we still feel at the approach of night, until we perceive that the sun was the real veil, drawn for a moment over countless splendours; and that he goes down into the sea, only to make way for 'Hesperus with all the host of heaven.' And so it is with death. Life is the day-star, the sun of our petty existence, veiling from our eyes the splendours of eternity. Death is the interpreter, the Revealer; our last breath is our apocalypse. But yet so controlled are we by our senses, that there is always an undefinable feeling of loneliness at sunset and at death. We are parting with the familiar, and going out

14

to the unfamiliar; for night, with all its starry splendours, is unknown to us. We know the gasjets of the ballroom and saloon; the electric arcs in the theatre. We never see the countless suns of the Universe. And death is unfamiliar, with all our experience of its surroundings. We must pass through its gates to understand its tremendous revelations.

Evening in great cities

But to come back. I think the city twilights are the most pathetic of all. The sinking, yellow sun streaming along such great thoroughfares as Trafalgar square and the Strand in London; or down along the Champs Elysées in Paris, and lingering on window, or column, or roof, has an aspect of extreme loneliness, emphasized by the little, twinkling eyes of the starjets or arcs, in café or restaurant, or even beneath the solemn trees. Man is summoned from labour to rest; and if one can pass by what he sees is the evening amusement of those 'whose lines are cast in pleasant places,' and watch the proletariat, the weary, bent, and broken masses of humanity, shuffling by with hod or mattock on shoulder, and probably envying the 'elect of the earth' who sit within their gorgeous clubs or cosy corners in the fashionable restaurant; and then follow them further to their foul haunts in byestreet or tenement house, and think of all the squalor and destitution and low mental and moral environments, one regrets that sunlight or twilight should pierce through and reveal the surroundings of toiling humanity; and would wish rather for the merciful darkness of winter that seems more in keeping with, and certainly covers more effectually, the sordid aspect which Life turns towards her suffering and unhappy children.

An island prison

The thought broke suddenly upon me, nor can I remove the haunting fascination of it to this day, one summer evening, very many years ago. It was not in a great city, but on a sunny island, 'a summer isle of Eden,' which by some tasteless ingenuity, had been made a penal settlement. A mission was being conducted there by regulars from the city; and we had been invited over to hear the convicts' confessions. It was pretty late when we finished; and, on our way to dinner, we had to pass through the dormitory, or sleeping apartments of the prisoners. It was just five o'clock; and the summer sun was streaming across the bay, lighting up the headlands all around, and the deep hulls of the ships, and casting great long shadows of buildings, and masts, and wooded promontories across the darkening sea. All was sunshine and life, and sweetness without; all was darkness and desolation here. For we saw but strong cages, tier over tier, walls and partitions of corrugated iron, and a net of strong wire, or iron in front of each cage, through which alone, the little air, and the little light from the outer hall penetrated. Each cell was eight feet by four, and each, even at that early hour, on that sweet summer evening, had its human occupant. Some were in bed; others sat wearily on the wretched wooden stool, and stared, like wild beasts at us; all were locked in. It was a human menagerie. I have often seen prisoners since then, even under worse circumstances. But somehow, these wire cages haunted my imagination. And then we stepped, free and unembarrassed, and honoured by the very warders, who held in their hands the keys of these human cages. The summer sun was oppressive in its heat and light. A pleasure steamer, well filled with all the fashion and style of a great city, panted by. A band was playing. No one gave a thought to the entombment of these fellow-mortals, just a few yards away.

A monastery

Some evenings later, I, too, was locked in at a comparatively early hour in some such solemn twilight as I loved. It was at a Cistercian monastery. The bells had ceased their interminable tolling, the rumbling of the organ was hushed; the pattering of feet had ceased; the very birds, as if respecting the Trappist rule, were silent. I sat and looked out across the darkening twilight at the white statues glimmering against the deep background of pines and laurel. If there be any spot on earth where there is peace, and rest, surely it is here. Some day a tired world will demand monasticism as a luxury, or a necessity. But that was not my thought as I sat there, and put my hand on some such work of Catholic philosophy, as the *Imitation,* or the *Soliloquia* of St. Augustine. My thoughts swiftly reverted to the penal settlement on the 'Isle of Eden,' and the cages, and their occupants. What an enormous gulf separated one condition from the other. There the one feeling uppermost was the degradation of

17

humanity; here, you experienced its elevation. It was the nadir and zenith of the race. And yet, the conditions of life did not differ so much. Nay, so far as physical comfort or enjoyment, the prisoners are much better off than the monks. The latter rise earlier, have much coarser and more meagre fare, work harder, keep perpetual silence, sleep on harder couches, submit to greater humiliations. And yet, there is the whole width of the horizon of heaven between them. There you pitied, or compassionated; here you are reverent and envious. Despair seemed to hover over the prison; but it is the wings of angels that lift the fringe of the pines that sentinel the mountain abbey.

Aut pati aut mori

But, there is something more curious even than this. I should not like to say that those poor, squalid prisoners would gladly exchange their lot with the monks. That is doubtful. But there can be no doubt that the monks, if called upon, would assume the garb, and chains of the felon; and in the terrible transmutation, experience only the greater joy. And the attraction would be, – the very degradation, and contempt, and loss of caste and honour, which is the peculiar lot of the convict. Does the world deem this credible? Well, we have proofs. If saints seek contempt, as ordinary mortals seek honours, if they have regarded themselves as the peripsema, and offscouring of humanity; if they have begged to be laid on ashes in their dying moments; or that they may be privileged to die on dunghills, remote from all human observation; if a

18

Vincent de Paul did go down to the galleys, and suffer the cannon-ball to be riveted to his ankles, as you can see in that famous picture by Bonnat; why may not all this be repeated, when the spirit and teachings of Christianity are the same; and when from countless human hearts made invincible by charity rises ever and ever that prayer of St. Teresa, '*Aut pati aut mori*'?

The immutability of Hope

I wonder is the secret to be discovered in that saying of Emerson's, 'The hope of man resides in the private heart, and what it can achieve by translating that into sense. And that hope, in our reasonable moments is always immense, and refuses to be diminished by any deduction of experience!' But that immutability of hope, my dear philosopher of Concord, demands the monk or the saint, or some such childlike and unspoiled temperament, as thine own. The 'deductions of experience' point all the other way. To keep one's heart unhardened until death is the achievement of a saint. Every stroke of the hammer of experience tends to anneal it. The two great impulses of Nature, even in its lowest forms, are self-preservation and reproduction, and both demand the wisdom of the serpent more than the meekness of the dove. And these impulses are accentuated and intensified by experience. Every man stands solitary, with all other men's hands against him. He must fight for existence. Failure, defeat, is the one hell to be dreaded. Success is the supposed Elysium. Nay, all our modern systems of education tend thitherward. For what is all this terrible and complicated

19

apparatus of education intended? What is the meaning of all this competition, rivalry, gaining of prizes etc.? What but the preparation for the greater struggle? And struggle means rivalry; and rivalry, enmity. For one alone can attain supremacy. And that one must be thou and no other. How are the best feelings of the heart translated into sense here?

Philanthropy

Nay, in such a struggle, where the watchword appears to be, 'We neither ask, nor give quarter!' would not the uncontrollable impulses of the heart be the great traitors? Could there be any hope of success for a man, who would be, above all things, generous, compassionate, self-sacrificing, kind? It is all right for you, my Croesus-friend, whom I see labelled 'multi-millionaire and philanthropist'! You can be lavish now, as much as you please. Nay, you must get rid of much of that glittering ballast, else it will sink your stately argosy. For gold is a weighty metal, you know; and you cannot steer well the ship of your fortunes, so long as you have so much of a dead weight in the hold. But 'philanthropist'? It is a pretty euphemism; and I don't like to quarrel with it. But I should have liked to know how you fared in the good ship Argo, as you set out in pursuit of the golden fleece. For I notice that Jason was very generous, and considerate, and pious to the gods, after his many adventures and trials. He built a splendid mausoleum to the island king whom he accidentally killed; and sacrificed a sheep or two, after he, in consort with the amiable enchantress,

20

Medea, had strewn the waters of the Euxine with the dismembered remains of the young Absyrtus.

Collegium Christi

I will suggest something to you, 'multi-millionaire and philanthropist,' which may obviate such expiations by suspending the possibility of your errors, at least for a lustrum. What would you think of building and endowing a new species of educational institution, to be called the Collegium Christi? It will have for its motto, 'S'effacer,' and 'Bear ye one another's burdens' may be inscribed over the lecture rostrums in the class-halls. It shall have all the latest appliances of science for the further conquest of Nature, and advancement of mankind. The extirpation of disease, the destruction of social evils, the bridging of the mighty gulf between rich and poor, the lifting up of fallen humanity, the study of criminology from the standpoint of Christ, the ventilation of grievances not as subjects for parliamentary eloquence, but as subjects to be grappled with, and destroyed and removed – these shall form the curriculum of studies. We shall by no means exclude the pagan ideals. You may have busts of Crates and Cincinnatus, but not of Croesus; Minerva and Apollo may grace your corridors, but the long perspective must not be bounded by glittering idola of Mammon and Plutus. For the former are merely symbols, and alas! rarely pass beyond the symbolic state. But these latter are the dread divinities that haunt the steps of mankind from the cradle to the grave.

Masked faces

But it is quite clear that to yield to heart-impulses and generous emotions is to court failure in the struggle for existence which has become with us synonymous with the struggle for wealth. Life is a masked ball, ending in success or failure. If you raise your domino, you might as well order your carriage, droskhy, or cab, and go home. You have revealed your identity, and the revelation is fatal. Unknown you might have moved safely among the unknown. But when everyone else knows you, whilst they remained unrevealed, what chance have you? You have lifted your visor in the tournament, and exposed yourself to deadly blows. Yes, get away from the tumult as quickly as you can; and, with the experience of so terrible a lesson, get away amongst the world's *anonymi*, and hide yourself. Or take some other mask and wear it closely; and keep a close hand upon those traitorous, if generous emotions, which are the fatal gifts of your heritage. It is all very melancholy; yet it is consoling to know that men have still hearts to feel, and if they must stifle their appeals, they cannot altogether still their beatings. And, now and again, secretly and with misgivings, they may yield to the luxury of fine pure emotions without the danger of ultimate betrayal.

Unmasked

Hence if you want to know what a man really is, watch him alone in the company of children. Here he can show himself as he really is, because, here he has nothing to fear, and nothing to gain. Elsewhere, even in the society of his intimates and relations, he cannot reveal himself. Brother is a mystery to brother; and father to child. In the drawing-room, in the council chamber, in the club, in the easy undress of an after-dinner, one would suppose that men are off their guard, and wear their hearts on their sleeves. No! assuredly no! wherever there is something to dread, the petals of the soul close in, as the petals of flowers at the coming of night; and open reluctantly only when the light appears again. What a history of mankind in miniature is that little story of a certain Queen-Regent of France, who was down on her knees, groping around with her hands and feet, playing Bo-peep with her little children in the nursery, amidst shouts, and shrieking and laughter! Suddenly the ambassador of a great state is announced. The mother stands at once erect, and is transformed into the regent; stately, stiff, and ceremonious, she steels her face against even a smile. That must be impenetrable – the domino is suddenly pulled down. She speaks in riddles, and answers in enigmas. She watches every line of his face to read it. She heeds not his words. They mean nothing. So too with him. He is studying her eyes, her features. Both are playing a part; and both know it. They separate with mutual compliments, and distrust. He goes back to his Cabinet, and mutters, 'A clever woman.' She goes back to her nursery, and resumes her play with her children. Here is the whole world in miniature.

Pitiable! Yes, perhaps so! But, *que voulez-vous?* You have outgrown your childhood; and mankind has got out of its nursery and small clothes. You talk pitifully of the world's childhood, of its myths, and legends, and superstitions. You speak of its heroes as of great big children of generous hearts and narrow minds. Your twentieth centuried scientist is painfully like the grandiose hero of Locksley Hall:

I to herd with narrow foreheads, vacant of our glorious gains,
Like a beast with lower pleasures, like a beast with lower pains.

Yes! he has gone a step higher. He is illuminated. He has electric cars and – railway murders. He has romantic novels and – divorces. He has the Stock-exchange, and – suicides. We are moving at break-neck speed; and the wheel of existence revolves so rapidly, that few gain the summit of the tire; and many are precipitated into the mire below. Inequalities between rich and poor yawn every day wider than the chaos between Dives and Lazarus. But on the wheel must go. He would be reputed a madman, or what is worse, an obscurantist, who would cry, 'Slow down, O wheel of life, and let the fallen arise! There is room for all within you and around you! Slow down, or break into splintered wood and twisted iron in the end.'

From dawn to dark

One cannot help thinking of such things, when memory recalls that prison-cage and its occupants, and the long streamers of the yellow sun gilding all Nature with their beauty. But these are sombre reflections, twilight thoughts. For hath not the ever true Psalmist said, 'In the evening weeping shall have place; in the morning, gladness.' Yes, let us carry, if we can, the wild freshness of morning with us through the entire day. From the *Subhi Kazib,* the False Dawn, the morning twilight, when sleepy little birds wake up reluctantly, and ask each other, Is it day? to the *Subhi Sadik,* the True Dawn, when all the woods are vocal with the deep rich music of blackbirds and thrushes; from that dawn to the fuller solar light, when already Nature is sheltering itself from his rays; from that brilliance of morning to midday, when no sound is heard but the *Coo, Coo, Coo,* of the solitary ringdove, hidden away in deep umbrageous fastnesses; on to the evening twilight, with its call to rest; let us keep the heart of the morning with its gladness, and make of the melancholy of twilight, a palinode of the music of the dawn. For there is no night in these summer months, but a great ring of light, with a black agate in the centre. And even that is shot through with light waves from the faint auroras of the setting and the rising sun.

The colour blue

It is strange that Nature so fond of using her blue pigments in other ways, is slow to waste it upon her most

25

perfect handiwork, the flowers. She lavishes and squanders it with the most incontinent profusion on her two great fields of colour, the sky and the sea. But she is singularly economic in its use in the forest, the field, or the flower-garden. At least she only uses it on her tiniest creations – violets or pansies, or forget-me-nots. These latter, indeed, are the only really blue flowers; for there is a strong infusion of Tyrian and royal purple in the violet and the pansy. But who ever heard of a blue rose, or a sapphire tulip or dahlia? Nay, I am not betraying my ignorance. I know what wonderful things our modern gardeners can effect; and how by the aid of chemistry, they can obtain what colours they please in their flowers. But I am speaking of Mother Nature. I want to know why she economises that lovely colour here; and I want to know whether the 'grand old gardener and his wife,' had, without the aid of chemistry, which I suppose was then unknown, such a thing as a blue rose in the garden of Eden. And if not, why? It is an interesting speculation. Has Nature used all the pigments up in her skies and seas, so that none is left for her children? Well, there is a compensation. 'What is rare is dear,' said the old logic-treatise. And we cannot help loving the tiny, blue-eyed little children that look all so modest beside their regal and florid sisters.

Novalis' blue flower

I think this must be the reason why that truly mystical German poet, Novalis, chose a blue flower as his symbol of poetry; poetry, itself being the supreme art in which all others are combined. And this was no tiny childkin of Nature, peeping shyly out of a mass of broad leaves, but a great, tall, pearly garden-queen, with a mass of broad, glittering petals, and springing from the moist earth near a stream. 'Round it stood innumerable flowers of all kinds and colours, and the sweetest perfume filled the air. He saw nothing but the blue flower, and gazed on it long with nameless tenderness. At last, he was for approaching, when all at once it began to move and change; the leaves grew more resplendent, and clasped themselves around the waxing stem; the Flower bent itself towards him; and the petals showed like a blue spreading ruff, in which hovered a lovely face.' So after innumerable adventures and wanderings through lonely, if beautiful places, he found the object of his life's search, and lo! it was all but a dream. So, too, was his vision of the deep, blue river in which he, embodied in his hero, Heinrich, sunk, swallowed in the vortices; and beneath which he meets once more Matilda, who put a wondrous secret word in his mouth, and it pierced through all his being. He was about to repeat it, when someone called, and he awoke. He would have given his life to remember that word. What was it? The Blue Flower is Poetry. What is the Word?

'Europe and Christianity

It is not a little singular that such a thinker, dreamer, mystic, yet mathematician and realist, should be so little known even in his own country. Still more singular is it that we have never utilized his most powerful and pene-

27

trating work, *Europe and Christianity*. There is such a dearth amongst us, not of apologies (of these we have enough) but of poetic and philosophical presentments of the aspects of Catholicity that present themselves so attractively to fine, spiritual natures, that one would have supposed we would seize on so eloquent a picture of what the Church is, and does for humanity, by putting before it the most sacred and poetic ideals.* The fact

* 'Those were beautiful, brilliant days when Europe was a Christian land, – when one Christianity occupied the continent. Rightfully did the wise head of the Church oppose the insolent education of men at the expense of their holy sense, and untimely dangerous discoveries in the realm of knowledge... This great interior schism (Protestantism) which destroying wars accompanied was a remarkable sign of the hurtfulness of culture. The insurgents separated the inseparable, divided the indivisible Church, and tore themselves wickedly out of the universal Christian union through which, and in which alone, genuine and enduring regeneration was possible. Luther treated Christianity in general arbitrarily, mistook its spirit, introduced another letter and another religion, the sacred universal sufficiency of the Bible namely. With the Reformation, Christianity went to destruction. Fortunately for the old Constitution, a newly-arisen order, the Jesuits, now appeared, upon which the dying spirit of the hierarchy seemed to have poured out its last gifts. In Germany one can already point out with full certainty the traces of a new world, – a great time of reconciliation, a new golden age, a Saviour dwelling among men, under countless forms visible to the believers, eaten as bread and wine, embraced as the Beloved, breathed as air, and heard as word and song. The old Catholic belief was Christianity applied, become living. Its presence everywhere in life, its love for art, its deep humanity, the indissolubility of its marriages, its humane sympathy, its joy in poverty, obedience and fidelity, make it unmistakably a genuine religion. It is made pure by the stream of time; it will eternally make happy this earth. Shall not Protestantism finally cease, and give place to a new, more durable Church?' (*Extract from Novalis, quoted by Hofmer, who always maintains that Novalis was certainly a Catholic; and quotes a number of authorities to support the statement.*)

28

alone that is was selected by Schlegel for publication in the Athenæum, but suppressed by Goethe, is an eloquent argument in its favour; and if any thing were wanting to such an argument, its magnificent defence of Catholic devotion to our Blessed Lady, so detested by materialists and neo-pagans, like Goethe, should prepossess us in its favour. He is but one of the many non-Catholic poets, who have dreamed of perfect spiritual beauty, and found that dream realized in

Maria, lieblich ausgedrückt.

Novalis and Heine

There is a wide difference between Novalis, writing such hymns as this Fifteenth, and writing from a bed of sickness, with all the ghastly forerunners of death showing themselves in violent hæmorrhages, and his fellow-countryman Heinrich Heine, rising from his mattress-bed in the Rue d'Amsterdam, semiparalysed and almost blind, to make his way to the Louvre to pay his valedictory visit to the Venus de Milo. 'Alas!' so he thought the mutilated statue replied, 'how can I help you? Do you not see that I, too, am powerless and armless, as yourself?' It seems like an excess of affection – this farewell to the marble Aphrodite. There is no parallel to it, except in the prayer of Ernest Renan to Minerva in the Acropolis:

Je n'aimerai que toi. Je vais apprendre ta langue, désapprendre la reste. J'arracherai de mon coeur tout fibre qui n'est

29

pas raison et art pur... Le monde ne sera sauvé qu'en reve-
nant à toi, en repudiant ses attaches barbares. Courons,
venons en troupe.

But then, as with Venus, comes the minor note of despair:

> Tout n'est ici-bas que symbole, et que songe.

The critical faculty

Venus was of but little help to Heine; Minerva of less
help to Renan. But how strangely, and irregularly move
the minds of men! The German-Jew scoffs, like his
progenitors, – scoffs at everything sacred and holy. He
has one idol, and but one, – Napoleon. The Breton Catholic does not sneer. Herein he differs much from his
countrymen. He only laments. He bewails lost gods, and
present beliefs in the living and eternal divinity. Yet, it
may be doubted whether Voltairean gibes at Christianity
would do more harm than his pathetic mourning over
human credulity, although, in some mysterious manner,
his critical faculty cannot altogether subdue some secret
yearning after the spirit of faith which it has vainly exorcised. And lo! the Lutheran Novalis finds in Catholicity, although he never embraced it* 'the only saving
faith;' and thinks the Reformation a 'most unqualified
evil.' It only proves for the hundredth time that the impulses of a generous and pure heart are more than the
'artistic sense,' and lead farther and deeper than the
'critical faculty,' no matter how highly developed.

* See above statement, and authorities quoted by Hofmer.

Two brothers

Probably no more interesting conversation was ever heard than that which took place between Novalis on his death-bed, and his brother, Charles Hardenberg, and which eventuated in the conversion of the latter to Catholicity. These conversations, too, afterwards gathered up and embodied, became the famous book of which we have spoken, *Europe and Christianity*. Novalis has been styled the German Pascal; and it would seem as if he had some idea of constructing a great scheme of ethical and philosophical principles on the same lines as his great French compeer. Like the latter, he had to leave his scheme unfinished, with just such pithy and pregnant apothegms as would lead us to conjecture what might have been the grandeur of the completed work. But the above-named essay remains almost entire; and to such minds as have the taste for such things, and can follow this mystic through the intricacies of unfamiliar thoughts woven into untranslateable language, the work, which aroused Tieck and Schlegel's enthusiasm, might be found not altogether unworthy or useless. For we do need a certain airy and poetic vesture for the dry bones of doctrine; and Theology, if the Queen of the Sciences, needs to be draped in royal robes to attract the homage of her subjects, and the reverence of those who are not yet her vassals or ministers.

Poetry, absolute reality

'Poetry is absolute reality. This is the kernel of my philosophy. The more poetic, the truer.' How this profession of Novalis jars upon the senses of those who see nothing but facts, and hear nothing but arguments! How it chimes with the more Catholic idea, which protests there is always something higher than reason; and that something the *donum descendens desursum* from the Father of all light. Yes! faith and poetry are near akin. The mere reasoner will never touch the altitudes of the former; the mere scientist, nay even, the mere artist, can never reach the Pisgah-heights of the latter. There is something more than mere perceptions of judgment or taste; and there are places where these faculties or gifts have to play a very subordinate part. 'Credo, quia impossibile' is not unreasonable. It merely confesses a higher power, and a higher region of sentiment or thought. 'Poetry is absolute reality.' Yes, if it be the poetry, unsensual and transcendental, which penetrates beneath the surface of things, and sees their essence, which looks beyond Art to that which it embodies; which beholds man, the mystery, interpreted by God, the everlasting Reality; and which understands that the mysteries of life and time are explained by Death and Eternity!

Tolstoy's 'Resurrection'

Quite in contrast with that highly-mystical and spiritual temperament, as represented by Tieck, Fouqué, and Novalis is the dread realism of our day. Before the echoes of the Easter bells, ringing out their glad Alleluias have died away, we read that Tolstoy's *Resurrection* has been placed in the stage in London, and that its representation, mainly owing to the acting of the lady who took the part of Katusha in the novel, has been almost an unprecedented success. It is a sign of the times – the eternal drifting, drifting of the world from pure and lofty ideals; and its rapid descent towards the newly-awakened sympathy with all that is spiritually deformed and obscene. Fifteen years ago, ten years ago, five years ago, no manager dare put such a drama of vice and loathsomeness on the stage. The Public Censor would inhibit it, and public opinion, if it escaped his censure, would condemn it. To-day, people throng the theatres to witness the most loathsome and degrading spectacle of a woman that even such a lurid imagination as Zola's could conceive; and the change is explained by the argument that the spirit of Charity is now more abroad than ever; and that even the purest minds may sympathise with the fearful degradation to which womanhood may be reduced by the habit of vice.

Art for its own sake

Such a plea is too pitifully transparent. To permit an immoral and degrading spectacle on the score of morality, and to invite the virtuous and clean of mind to witness such grossness on the plea of awakening their sympathy, is too hollow a pretence to need refutation. Something else is needed, and it is forthcoming in the ancient formula: 'Art for its own sake, and Art, independent of morality.' This is intelligible. Once can argue with it. No one would waste ink in refuting the former defence. It is the final apology for realism. It is the ethics of materialism worked out to a logical conclusion. But Art for its own sake! How often we have heard it! How the changes have been rung upon it, in painting, in sculpture, in poetry! It is the religion, where 'there ain't no Ten Commandments'; and where licentiousness may revel without license. And Tolstoy's *Resurrection* is Art. There is no question of it. And Nehlúdoff and Maslova are as terribly real as the infernal princes in *Paradise Lost*; but alas! they represent passions, which are far more infectious and dangerous, because more human and common. It is, indeed, possible that their dreadful consequences may be a deterrent against vice; but the principle is an old one and a safe one: Is is better to attract towards the positive than repel from the negative. And it is doubtful if vice can ever be painted in such hideous colours as to exorcise the passions of mankind.

In a Dublin Gallery

But, Art for its own sake! Art as Teacher, because of its own intrinsic perfection; and because perfection of any kind is morality! This is a great and subtle heresy. I heard it once refuted by a parable, founded on fact.

A young student not enamoured of Art for its own sake, but anxious to see two things, – a certain painting of Turner's, and Burton's drawing of the head and face of Clarence Mangan, as he lay dead in the Meath Hospital, visited the National Gallery in Dublin. It was the old gallery, and this was many years ago. Having feasted his eyes on Turner, and sketched with a pencil roughly the head of the dead poet, he turned to depart. The gallery was well filled with sight-seers, – city-loungers, strolling from picture to picture, and from statue to statue; a few country-cousins staring with open mouths at the Art-nudities that filled up the centre of the gallery; here and there, a student copying; not a few others affecting art-studies, and standing before large easels, or unfolding massive portfolios. But the student's work was done, and he hastened to leave. Just as he stood at the head of the broad staircase, a lady with her two daughters came up the steps, with that eager look which people assume when they expect something delightful. The three stood on the top step, looked at the nude Venuses, and Apollos for a moment, seemed transfixed into marble themselves, so tense were their surprise and horror; and then with a simultaneous movement, they rushed down the staircase, and out into the open air.

Not modern, but right

'Obscurantists,' 'reactionaries,' 'prudes,' I fancy I hear someone saying. But let me suppose that that lady, and her two girls, brought suddenly from the sweet seclusion of a refined home, and with all kinds of modest and deli-cate ideas, did yield to such a clamour; and did go around, coolly and critically surveying the marble figures or plaster casts, could we consider it really a gain? It would be quite in accordance with all we read about the advance of education, the march of progress, the *Zeit-*

geist; but would we like it? Or rather would we not share the feelings of that student, who, on witnessing this glorious retreat of modest women, and all it conveyed more eloquently than the most impassioned oratory, did lift his hat on high, and mutter deep down in his heart: Thanks be to God?

Goethe and Novalis

Here was the fundamental difference between Goethe and Novalis. The former was a pagan, who worshipped Art for its own sake. The latter a Christian, who believed Art should be the handmaid of religion. To the former all the mediæval churches in Christendom were not worth a Greek torso dug from the ruins of the Acropolis; to the latter, these churches were not only monuments of faith, but temples whose sacred gloom, shot through and through by heavenly lights transfused through the consecrated figures of virgins and martyrs, made an aureole on the mosaic of the floor, and around the daily lives of countless multitudes who held that life had essential duties, but that their futures were safeguarded by the diligent combination of work and worship here. The former thought Christianity a development of priest-craft, happily checked and stayed by the Reformation. The latter, though a Lutheran, believed that the visible Church was the seamless robe of Christ, and that the capital crime of the Reformers was 'separating the inseparable, dividing the indivisible Church.' And hence, like his modern disciples, the former regarded the French Revolution as a 'truth, clad in Hellfire;' the latter, the logical outcome and consequence of the moral and intellectual libertinism which commenced in the Reformation.

Philosophy and Economy

And philosophy! How he loathes that mock-philosophy of France which, eliminating all that was gracious in the past, religion and enthusiasm and self-sacrifice, makes of the Universe a mill, and all the music of the spheres the rumble and clatter of machinery! And how he rises as on wings of light to a right conception of its sphere, as postulating for man a universe and surroundings congruous with his higher want and aspirations.

'Philosophy can bake no bread; but she can procure for us God, Freedom, Immortality. Which, then, is more practical: Philosophy or Economy?'

'Philosophy is properly Home-sickness; the wish to be everywhere at home.'

'The true philosophical act is self-annihilation. This is the real beginning of all philosophy; all requisites for being a disciple of philosophy point hither.'

'The first Man is the first Spirit-Seer; all appears to him as spirit. What are children but first men? The fresh gaze of a child is richer in significance than the forecasting of the most indubitable Seer.'

A new Europe

But, with all his sorrow over German Reformations, French Revolutions, and other disastrous signs of steady decadence in human affairs, he does not despond. He was too young and inexperienced to despair. It is only those who have reached the middle term of life that can afford to be pessimists. The young have the morning sun of gladness in their eyes; the old, the setting sun of tranquillity. The grey sky hangs above Life's meridian. Hence Novalis is hopeful. He believes we shall see 'a new Europe, an all-embracing, divine place.' When will it be? We cannot say. Only let us have patience. It will come; it must come.'

A century has gone by since he wrote these words; and who shall say his prophecy has been verified? Or where, if anywhere, can we look around and say that the dream of this Poet-Philosopher has come true?

SECTION II.

By the Sea

The problem suggested itself, and a possible solution one day two summers agone, as I sat in a cleft of red sandstone, in a cathedra, or chair, improvised by the action of the sea far down in what are known as the Diamond Rocks at a certain watering-place. It was out of the shadows of the cedars; and my limited horizon had faded out and lengthened into the boundless expanses of the ocean. There, beneath my feet, boiled the surges; and there was no break in the continuity of that mighty element, which tossed up yellow flecks on these rocks, washed the shores of Labrador out yonder, and hid in warm sunny nooks beneath the palms of Sorrento, or under the domes and minarets of Stamboul. Somehow one's mind expands with this glorious element, and the great dome of the sky leans down north, south, east, and west, unmarred and unlatticed by branches or foliage; whilst the constellations repeat their splendours in the false firmament that is created beneath these dark-blue waves. It is a place where one may think a good deal and without interruption, unless nature is in a capricious temper, and is determined to woo your mind from abstract thought to her ever-attractive interplay of wind and wave.

Nature not Solitude

I had come down from another popular resort on the same coast, along the savage sea-line that is jagged and bitten into mercilessly by the unrestrained Atlantic; and here, on the warm summer mornings, before the visitors at the Hotel had finished their morning papers and correspondence, I had Nature, in her most lovely and attractive and terrible aspects, all alone to myself.

Yet, it was not solitude. How could it be when there was beauty and music all around, – the savage, untamed beauty of sea and rock and cliff; and the more tender beauty of deep seapools here and there in the crevices – seapools clear and green as the most fleckless emerald, and in their depths purple molluscs, whose deep, rich Tyrian dyes contrasted with the limpid water; and wonderful algæ of every shape and colour, floating and coiling and waving their long, cool flags, as the wind rippled the waters around them? And lest there should be aught to mar the freshness and sweetness and purity of these tiny lakelets, twice a day the great Mother-Sea poured in her living waters in deep channels, and flushed the cisterns with foam, which melted into glittering globes, and sweetened and purified the rock-wells down to their lowest depths. And sea-gulls gleamed white and gray above the surges; and speckled sea-swallows dipped and flashed here and there from wave to rock, and from rock to wave.

There could be no solitude here, for voices were ever calling, calling to you; and you had to shade your eyes from the glare of sunlit foam, that not only dazzled and blinded at your feet, but floated up in a kind of seadust that filled all the air with sunmists, and was shot through and through with rainbows that melted and appeared again, and vanished, as the sunlight fell, or the wind caught the smoke of the breakers and flung it back against the steel-blue, darkened sea without. Far up along the coast, you could see the same glorious phenomenon – a fringe of golden foam breaking helplessly against iron barriers; and, here and there where a great rock stood alone and motionless, cut loose from the mainland by centuries of attrition, you might behold cataract after cataract of molten gold pouring out and over it, covering it for a moment in a glittering sheet of waters, and then diminishing into threads of silver as the spent waves divided into tiny streamlets and fell. It was again the eternal war of Nature, the aggressive sea, flinging its tremendous tonnage of waters on the land; and the patient rocks, washed and beaten and tortured, for ever turning their patient faces to the sea.

Rest

Why does not all the world come to Ireland, at least for the few days of quiet breathing and torpor which Summer brings, and which even the most exacting Shylock of the modern world must allow? If I were a Croesus

41

philanthropist, such as I have already described, I would take from out all the factories and workshops of the world these pale mechanics, these anæmic and wasted women, and bring them here. I would take them from the stifling atmosphere where they breathe poison, and fill their lungs with strong, clean, salt air from the sea. For the rumble and thunder of machinery, I would give them the ever-soothing sounds of winds and waves. For the smell of oil and rags, and the odours of streets and slums, I would give them the intoxicating perfume of winds fragrant from their march over purple heather and yellow broom, and the subtle scents that breathe from seaweed washed with brine, and exhaling its sweetness and strength. And I would say to them: 'Here! rest and forget! Plunge in these breakers; read, and pause, and think all day! The cares of life have no place here. They have "folded their tents like the Arabs." There is nothing over you here but the blue dome of heaven and the Eye of God looking through.'

A Briton

The English have long ago discovered these nooks of Paradise on the Irish Coast. They have so completely monopolised one or two down there in the Kingdom of Kerry that they feel quite resentful since the natives have found out these beauty spots, and are actually courageous enough to demand a right to share them. And here on this wild coast you will see a solitary Briton, a bewildered and almost panic-stricken mortal, palefaced, thinly-bearded, spectacled, with the field glass slung around his shoulders and something like an alpenstock in his hand. He looks rather fearfully around. He is outside civilisation, and he does not know what is going to happen. He is quite astonished at the temerity of these young gentlemen in white flannels, and these young ladies in tennis costumes, swinging their bats gaily, as they mount the declivity towards the broad plateau above the sea. By and by, his nerves cool down, and if he can pick up courage enough to answer your kindly greeting, you will find him a bright, clear, intelligent soul. He is just come from the Bodleian, or the British Museum. The smell of books and mummies hangs around him. He, too, needs the sea.

Bronzed and ruddy Irish

But all these bronzed and ruddy Irish, with health and life in every movement, feet that spring lightly from the turf, clean, ruddy bodies, as you see, when they plunge from the rock or spring-board and cut their way, like natives of the element, across the sea; what are they doing here? Taking their holidays? There are no holidays in Ireland; for every day is a holiday. We take the best out of life, and laugh at the world pursuing its phantoms across the weary wastes bleached with the bones of the unsuccessful and the fallen. We do not teach the philosophy of the schools well; but we practise the philosophy of life perfectly. So thinks evidently my statuesque Englishman, whose nerves are somewhat startled by our exuberant spirits. So think these German lads, who, amazed at Irish generosity, believe the donors of these

43

innumerable sixpences millionaires, although the donors may be as poor as themselves. So think these two lonely Italian brothers, who vend their pretty, artistic paper-weights at fabulous prices. They are Garibaldians, if you please, brought up to believe that a government of priests is the worst in the world. They have been beaten into orthodoxy by the old Irishwoman, who feeds them, as if they were her own children, and thinks she has a right, therefore, to chastise their irreligion. But all carry back to their homes the idea that the Irish are the freest, gayest, most irresponsible people on the surface of the earth.

A Summer evening

It is evening here. The sun has just gone down over there towards America, with all the pomp and splendour of cloud curtains and aerial tapestries; and the sea swings calm, acknowledging the prescriptive right of the vesperal time to peace. The wealthy classes, who have just dined; the more modest people, who have just had tea; are all gathered pell-mell here before the handsome villas that crest the summit of these cliffs above the sea. Just here, inside the seawall, between two priests, sits an aged Arch-bishop, the weight of eighty winters bending his broad shoulders as he looks across the darkening bay, and thinks of many things. Undeterred by rank or splendour, for there is a kind of glorious communism here, crowds of young lads and girls throng the seawall. A German band is playing Strauss and Waldteufel waltzes. But it is not dance music these Irish want. They demand the *Lieder* of the Fatherland. For every penny they give for a waltz, they will give sixpence for a German song. A young Bavarian, fair-haired, blue-eyed, will oblige them. And there above the Atlantic surges, on this wild coast, the strange, sweet melodies, learned far away in some woodman's hut in the Black Forest, are entrancing Irish hearts, which understand not a single articulate guttural or labial of the foreigner, but feel the magic of the music stealing their senses away. And then the strangers reciprocate. And a hundred voices sing. 'Come back to Erin, mavourneen, mavourneen,' to the accompaniment of violoncello and bassoon.

A family party

Passing along the corridor of my hotel that night on the way to my own room, I was accosted by a friend. After a few minutes conversation, he invited me to his room. Oysters and champagne? No. A game of Nap? No. A whole family, three generations of them, were gathered into the father's bedroom. They were saying their night-prayers before separating for the night. The aged grandmother was reciting the first decade of the Rosary, as we entered. We knelt. When she had finished the decade, she looked around and said: 'Alice, go on.' Alice was a tiny tot of seven summers. She promptly took up the recitative, repeated the form of the meditation, as found in Catholic prayer-books, and slowly and sweetly gave out the decade to the end. The grandmother looked around again, and called out: 'Go on, Willie.' Willie was the father, a grey-haired man of fifty-seven. To the mother's imagination he was but the child she had carried in her arms half a century ago. Willie finished, and the aged mistress of ceremonies called out, now a grand-child, now the mother, until all was ended. Then the children kissed 'good-night,' and departed. Across the yard, which is also our garden,

> All night have the roses heard
>   The flute, violin, bassoon;
> All night has the casement jessamine stirred
>   To the dancers dancing in tune.

They kept me awake

> Till a silence fell with the waking bird,
>   And a hush with the setting moon.

Is this the solution?

And this was the subject of my meditation the following morning, as I sat in my perch there above the sea. Here is the world's great secret solved. Here is the dream of the gentle mystic, Novalis, realised. Not that the scheme has yet rounded to absolute perfection here. The material and subordinate element has to be developed as yet to supplement the spiritual forces that are alive and active. But all the possibilities of such a perfect scheme of human happiness as Novalis dreamed of, are here – Nature with all her magic beauty; Art in embryo, but with every promise of speedy and perfect development, and Religion, holy and mysterious mother, overshadowing all. Comfort without wealth, perfect physical health with-out passion, ambition without cruelty, love without desire, the enjoyment of life without forgetfulness of eternity, the combination of spiritual and temporal interests, gaiety without levity, the laugh that never hurts, the smile that is never deceptive, clean bodies, keen minds, pure hearts, – what better world can philosopher construct, or poet dream of?

A shrine

I choose this watering-place rather than the former as both the type and theatre of what we may expect when some great constructive spirit comes along from eternity to harmonise apparently rival elements, and bring all into the perfect symmetry of a *Civitas Dei in terra*. Because here was a leaven of worldliness and pleasure; there religion dominated and interpenetrated everything. That place seems more like a shrine than a fashionable resort. If one did not know otherwise, he might mistake that lonely hamlet, undistinguished except for a few monster hotels, there on the brown moorland, seven miles from a railway station, and with only the thin sea-line in the distance, for a La Salette or a Lourdes. How otherwise shall you account for those grey-haired priests waiting from five o'clock these summer mornings for the sacristy door to be opened? How will you explain the constant succession of masses at different altars, from five o'clock to ten, each mass followed by an immense and fervent congregation; how will you interpret the constant stream of devout worshippers that passes into that church all day long, to make visits, follow the Stations of the Cross, recite the Rosary, &c.? Pleasure-seekers and health-seekers? Where are they? God-seekers and soul-seekers rather, for never a mission or retreat was attended with such passionate fervour and piety, as these well-dressed worshippers exhibit, as they seem to grudge the time at the Spa or at the sea, or on the far cliffs, as so much stolen from God.

Aran-na-Naomh

And just there, look! Across that bight of sea sleep the three islands that link us with the past, and whose traditions, were we otherwise, would shame us. They are *Aran-na-Naomh*, Arran of the Saints, where rests the dust of thousands whose lives were heroic. You are at the end of civilization and the beginning of heaven. There is not in the world so savage a spot as that where I stand. It is a huge plateau or shelf of limestone rock, pitted and marked by immense holes where the eternal rains have worn the soft limestone. Beneath my feet the devouring sea is thundering and bellowing through deep sea-caves where all the finny monsters of the sea might hide forever, and never be found. There is no gentleness here! It is not

> The blind wave feeling round his long seahall
> In silence

you hear, but the savage waves leaping and tearing with aggressive fury through every vantage point created by their ceaseless and never-ending attacks. It is a place for the hermit and the saint; and mark you, O world-dreamer

and farseer, the hermit and the saint must again resume
their rightful places in the economy of new orders and
systems! You cannot do without them. They symbolise
the rest and the gracious peace which the world will ever
stand in need of.

Human and Divine

But here, in this more fashionable place, there is something more of the human element; and it makes things
more interesting to a student of humanity, although they
may not reach such sublimity in idea or feeling. And as
it is this commingling of the human and divine that will
form the great principle or organic constituent of the
commonwealth that is to be, it makes an apter subject
for study than society where religion not only predom-
inates, but is everything.

For it is easy to solve the problem, Humanity alone.
And it is easy to solve the problem, Religion alone. But
to combine both in one great republic of reason, each
fitting in and harmonising with the other, with no repel-
lent principles underlying the structure of either, but both
co-operating to develop all that is best in nature, and to
eliminate all that is evil – here is the great problem to be
solved by some mastermind under the distinctly unfavour-
able circumstances of modern European life, or to be
evolved naturally from some such condition of society as
that which we have described, and which seems to be the
prerogative of this Catholic land of ours.

Tolstoy and Ibsen

I think all unbiassed minds, anxious for this union of
culture and religion, would choose this our country for
the experiment. All conditions seem happily placed for
the working out of the gigantic problem. It would be no
place certainly for a Voltairean scoffer, for the omni-
scient yet agnostic scientist, or for a more modern Ibsen-
ite, who would pin his faith to the prophets of naturalism.
I am quite sure that if I were to place this book of Tolstoy's in the hands of any young girl who is now sitting
on these crags that overhang the Atlantic, she would fling
it into the sea before she had read a dozen pages. I am
quite sure if I told any of these ecclesiastics, who mingle
so freely amongst their people here, the story of Parson
Brand, he would at once say that the stoning and sub-
sequent interment of that idealist in an avalanche were
richly deserved. For, somehow, eccentricities of any kind
are laughed out of court here; and for a sentimental
people, it is wonderful how they have caught and re-
tained that sense of the *juste milieu* that lies at the bottom
of all reason and all order.

Introspection and neurotic literature

The two things that seem to have preserved the buoyancy
of this people hitherto are the total absence of the habit
of introspection; and their ignorance of the neurotic literature of the age. It is quite true that their feelings with
surprising and painful quickness, leap from depression to
exaltation and *vice versa*; but this swift succession of

feeling is emotional, and not intellectual. Except on the occasion of confession, in which they are strongly advised to be brief and definite, they never look inward to scrutinize motives or impulses. They know nothing of psychological analysis of themselves; and they are content to measure others by what they see, without desiring to unveil and pry into the hidden sanctuary where rests that Holy of Holies – the human soul. And hence there can be no morbidity here. They look like children at the surface of things, and as these surfaces are mostly smooth, and it is only beneath there is the ruffling of tempests, they are content to take life even so, and say, All is revealed, and all is well.

The Welt-Schmerz

It is a negative constituent of happiness, too, that hitherto they have never heard of the strange modern literature that commencing with the morbid analysis of human thoughts and motives ends in revolting realism and dreary pessimism. They know nothing of the *Welt-Schmerz*, have never heard of Parson Manders or Rosmer Solness with his dreary verdict on his life: 'As I look backwards, I have really built nothing, and sacrificied nothing to be able to build;' Oswald Alving is as yet a stranger, and happily the sculptor Rubek with his Irene and Maia are unknown names. They would not class the creator of such types with Shakspere, even if they knew them. In fact, they are a healthy people, and just as they never will be taught to appreciate high venison or rotten Stilton, so, too, they have not reached as yet that intellectual status when nerves seem to be everything, and healthy thought is not only unrefined, but morbid. In fact, some one has called this country:

Mundus mundulus in mundo immundo.

Will it last?

Will all this last? Ah, there is the problem I am trying to solve here on this rockshelf above the immaculate sea. Will not the *Zeit-geist* come along and seize these island people, as it has seized the world without? How can we stop the process of the suns, or turn back the hand on the dial of time? And if education has to advance, as it is advancing by leaps and bounds, must not the literature of introspection and bad nerves and pessimism creep in gradually, and affect the whole mental and moral life of the country? And then, what becomes of your spiritual and physical health, and the beautiful happy balance and poise of faculties, neither enervated by disease, nor warped by intellectual misdirection? It is a big problem; and push it as far back as we like, it will loom up suddenly some day, and demand a solution, or an unmolested influence, such as we see unhappily bearing bitter fruit in other, and less favoured lands.

An Amiel or Senancour, impossible

It is hard to imagine such a revolution in a nation's ideas as this supposes; and, as I study this strange people here in their humid climate and surrounded by a misty and melancholy ocean; as I see them watching dreamily the sunsets over the western ocean, as only a poetic people may; dancing in ballrooms to-night until twelve o'clock; reverently worshipping at the morning. Mass; returning to their hotels dripping brine from dress and hair; spending the day in excursions and amusements; but always ending it in the parish church; and, as I think you cannot move in any circle of society here, or change your location, or stir hand or foot without coming bolt upright against God; I conclude that a genius so varied and exalted will never long suffer itself to be linked with the spirit of the age or any other spirit of darkness; but will always rise above mere materialism on the wings of the poetic idea, and always keep within touch of reality through its moral and religious instinct. I doubt if Ireland will ever produce an Amiel, or a Senancour, or a Rousseau.

The Man of Letters

But the man of letters will come; and the man of letters will always set himself in opposition to what he is pleased to designate sacerdotalism. Literature and dogma have never yet been taught to go hand in hand. For literature has a dogmatic influence of its own; and believes its highest form to be didactic. Unlike Art, whose central

ciple is, Art for its own sake alone, Literature as-
..es, and in all ages, but more especially in modern
times, the privilege of 'guide, philosopher, friend' to the
world. Hence we find that the worst forms of literature are
excused on the ground that they teach a lesson. *Anna
Karénina, Resurrection, Ghosts, Lourdes, Rome, Paris,*
are all sermons, told with all the emphasis not of voice or
accent, but of a horrible realism, that affects one's nerves
more terribly than the most torrential eloquence. And
now that literature is pledged to preaching, it is doubtful
if it ever will drop the *rôle.* And so the man of letters will
come to Ireland, as he has come to France, to England,
to Germany, and with him the seven other spirits, Zeit-
geists, Welt-Schmerzes &c., to abide and take up their
home, or to be exorcised and banished summarily and
for ever.

The one enemy

And all the spirits have one enemy, and but one, – the
spirit of religion. This was the *L'Infâme* of Voltaire, who
dreaded it so much that he would banish from his republic of atheism even the ancillary arts of poetry and
music and painting. Everything that savoured of idealism,
and appealed to aught but the senses, was ruthlessly
ostracised. The fight in that unhappy country of his,
between the man of letters and the priest, between literature and dogma, lasts to this day, with such lurid
manifestations, as French Revolutions, Carmagnoles, &c.
Then came the man of letters in the shape of the scientist,
also banishing from human thought everything that

savoured of the Ideal, everything that could not be peered at in a miscroscope, or examined in a test-tube. He has passed, too, but left his mark on the religious tone of England. Now, comes the man of letters, with his religion of Humanity, from the steppes of Russia to the Scandinavian mountains, and thence to the mud-dykes of Holland; and he, too, comes in the name of religion, with priests, and ritual and ceremonies – above all with Dogma – the Dogma, that man is supreme and there is no one like him in heaven or on earth.

This people of Destiny

And I can forecast the time when this people of destiny, here by the wild seas of the north, and right in the gangway of the modern world, will have to face and examine the dogma of this modern literature. Nay, I can see certain vacillations and soul-tremblings under the magic of the sweet and delicious music of language, attuned and attenuated in accordance with the canons of modern, perfect taste. But I know that the sturdy character of the people, stubborn after their eight hundred years of fight, and their religious instincts which nothing can uproot, and their power of adapting all that is best in life with all that is useful for eternity, and above all, their sense of humour, will help them after the first shock to vibrate back towards their traditional and historical ideals, and finally settle down into the perfect poise of reason and religion combined. They never will accept literature as dogma; but they may turn the tables, and make their dogmatic beliefs expand into a world-wide literature.

Literature our ally

That is just the point. Can literature be made our ally, as it has hitherto been our enemy? Are literature and Catholic dogma irreconcilable? He would be a bold man, who would assert it, with Calderon and Dante before his eyes. But we do not sufficiently realise and understand that poetry, romance, art, – everything that idealises, is on our side. If Voltaire banished from the republic of letters everything that savoured of chivalry, enthusiasm, poetry, heroism, it is quite clear that these must have been recognised as the allies of religion. And when the inevitable reaction took place, one by one these ambassadors were recalled, and at length religion was accepted and enthroned in the very places where she had abdicated or been expelled. Sir Walter Scott's Waverley novels prepared the way for the Tractarian movement, and became its initial impulse; and Tieck, Novalis, the Schlegels, who formed the romantic school in Germany, prepared men's minds for Catholicism by recalling the ancient glories that filled every city of Europe with cathedrals, and the galleries of Italian churches with priceless and immortal Art.

A student

Just as I scratched these words in pencil in a note-book, I became aware of a figure beneath me, standing in a hesitating way on a great shelf of rock that sloped down into a crystal pool of sea-water. It was a young student, and I thought: 'He wants to bathe, and no wonder. Yonder bath of crystalline purity, improvised by Mother Nature, would tempt a hydrophobic patient. He is shy about disrobing in my presence; so I will leave him alone with the luxury. No! he did not want to bathe. He wanted a chat. Might he take the liberty, &c., &c.? By all means. He was very young, but I am not one of these who believe that to be a young man is a crime. If the ideas of youth have not an autumnal mellowness, at least they have all the freshness of spring. It is good and wholesome to talk with the young, not for what they may learn, but for what they impart. It is good to see young hopes unfolding, and young ambitions ripening, and young eyes looking boldly and unflinchingly along the road which we have trodden, where we have leaped some pitfalls, and fallen into others, and have now very little left of the weary journey but its dust, and sweat, and languour. And my young friend was buoyant. He wanted to know everything, and to try everything. The red light of the dawn was on his wings, as he tried to soar in the empyrean.

Souls

All was on his side, – youth, enthusiasm, health, hope; he felt he lacked but one thing – knowledge. Not wisdom, mind! What youth ever deemed he lacked wisdom? But he felt there were certain things hidden from him and but dimly revealed; and he wanted to tear away the veil, and see them in all their naked truth. He intended leaving Ireland and going abroad. It did not matter where. He wanted work, and arduous work and difficulties and trials; otherwise he could never find his manhood. Missionary life in Ireland is merely running a knife through a cheese. You could not call that work, could you now? But he felt (he was modest enough to admit it), that the difficulties he sought to confront and conquer were of an intricate nature, inasmuch as they sprang from souls; and he was reverent enough to say, that man's soul, be it the soul of a poet or a hind, is a kind of Holy of Holies, only to be approached with a certain awe, and, above all, with the shoes off the feet, by which I think he meant purity of intention. And, furthermore, as it was not likely that he would go amongst savages to teach them to wear blankets, and abstain from roast baby-fingers, he thought that the souls he wished to conquer might need reasoning with, if one were ever to understand the crypts and labyrinths that wound their dark and devious ways through modern human thought.

Literature a general confession

Would it not be well to make a study of such souls, to try to understand them; above all, to get on to their standpoint, and to see through their eyes? How do they deal with all these complex situations in which men will find themselves, in spite of every effort to keep themselves free, or disentangle themselves? And, surely, if progress means passing out from the homogeneous to the heterogeneous, and if this is the most progressive of ages, the multitude of thoughts that vex, emotions that stir, principles that guide, passions that mislead, must be beyond counting. But these we can never understand, so utterly different are our own surroundings, unless we have the faculty of going out of ourselves and entering the minds of others. Experience alone can thoroughly teach this; but experience of this kind comes to one priest in a million. How then shall we know these secrets? Well, the literature of the world is the mind of the world placed articulately before us. Literature is the world's general confession, because it is the revelation of certain minds, which owe all their success to the fact that they have caught up the spirit of the age, and rendered its voiceless agony articulate.

Ennui – the evil of the Age

Now the malady of this age is Ennui – the eternal getting tired of, and wearying of monotony, – in religion, art, science, and literature itself. Heresy is ennui of the sameness of rite, ceremonial, and prayer. Hence, we see many, who have entered the Church from emotional, or æsthetic impulses, very soon tire of such monotony and drift back to the 'Variety Theatre' of their youth.

Furthermore, infidelity is the delight of despair. There is a certain paroxysm of pride in defying or denying God. Milton has put it in the souls of the rebel angels. It is the ecstasy of the lost. Dante never understood it. Hence, amongst all his reprobate, there are no defiant souls. All are despairful or admit the justice of their punishment. Why? Because infidelity did not exist in Dante's time; and to his great Catholic mind it was inconceivable. But if any Dante or Milton could arise now, he could impersonate another phase of the malady in the *ennuyées* and the defiant. Yes, the passion for change, and the revolt of the intellect, are amongst the many symptoms of this overwrought and frenzied age.

Systems, and Dogma

It is one of the reasons, my young student-friend, why theories and systems are always acceptable to the human mind; dogmas, never! The former place no shackles on the intellect. You can move easily to and fro beneath them, or cast them aside altogether. But dogma binds the intellect, and the intellect chafes beneath it. You must break the neck of *Non serviam* before the head bows beneath the keystone of the arch. And strangely enough, this is just what modern science, nay, even what modern literature, is doing, it may be unconsciously. The man of letters is the Samson of the New Revolution. He preaches man's perfectibility, and shouts Liberty, Fraternity, Equality, whilst allowing his axe to fall on his unhappy victims. And the world will one day awake from the horrid dream, and demand a return to common sense, and a sane understanding of man's relations with the Universe. The hermits in the desert of science must be also visionaries; and the apparitions are for the most part diabolic.

Common sense and repose

What then have we to teach the world, that is, if the world will condescend to listen? Simply a return to common sense and a little repose of the spirit. To this end, men must seek God and Nature a little more, self and society a little less. The great Master and Model, after His day's labour in squalid towns, or along the dusty roads of Judea, went up at night into the mountain to pray. Even He sought solitude as a balm and sedative for tired brain and nerves. Hence I hold that monasticism sprang from a necessity of Nature, as well as from the decree of God. The deserts of Nitria and Libya were little paradises of peace after the maddening whirl and excitement of Greek or Roman cities. But even in the desert, even here, my young student friend, beside the barren sea, we must keep away from analysis and introspection; and maintain our souls on the perfect poise which we witness everywhere in Nature. Mark the swing of that sea, the return of that star. All is obedient to law. There is no liberty anywhere. The tides are chained to the moon; the star runs in its appointed groove. They do not ask the why or the wherefore. They are content with their equilibrium. Why should man's mind alone be lawless and untamed?

A little Drama

My young student did not see the bearing of the parallel on the question he had originally propounded. But he will later on. He went his way, I am afraid, dissatisfied. And immediately beneath me, fifty feet or so and on the shelf of rock where I had seen him, stood a youth and a young girl. They were conversing earnestly. And then the former knelt on the rock, and with some sharp instrument, cut deep into the stone, his companion watching intently. They too, went their ways; and I was curious enough to see what he had cut in the rock. It was a circle, within which were the magic letters A. and R. It was the first act in a little drama. Next morning we were horrified at breakfast to hear that a young law student from Dublin had just been drowned in the bay. He had been an expert swimmer, had slept late, and essayed to swim across the neck of waters that connected the inner bay with the ocean. He had been seen to cross half way over, then to fling up his hands, and sink. There was no help at hand. All the great swimmers had gone back to their hotels.

Acts II. and III.

There was great gloom all day over the little place. In the evening I was in my usual perch on the cliffs. The sun was setting amidst all the gorgeous magnificence of a clouded, but not darkened sky. One solitary figure fifty feet beneath me, watched it. Then I saw that infinitely pathetic human gesture, the secret wiping away of a tear. She turned, and bending down, she traced with the sharp end of her parasol the letters on the rock; and then the round circle that clasped them, several times. There was no mistaking Act II. in the little drama. 'Here last evening we stood, and here, &c., &c. And now I am alone, and he –' An hour later I entered the parish church to say my evening prayer. My student was making the Stations of the Cross; and the young bereaved one was kneeling at the feet of *Christus Consolator*. I did not hear a word: but I knew what she was saying. They were the words of Martha and Mary. 'Lord, if Thou hadst been there. But now I know that whatever Thou askest of God, He will grant thee.' What did she want? His poor body was out at sea, half-eaten by sharks. That she should never see more. What, then? What these Irish, student or soulfriend, seem to be ever dreaming about – the soul.

The Amen of the Universe

Here was a direct exemplification of that saying of Novalis: 'Absolute love, independent of the heart, and grounded upon faith, is religion. Love can pass through absolute will, into religion. We become worthy of the highest being only through death, atoning death.' To a superficial mind it sounds sentimental. We must understand how deeply those mystics felt, as well as how serenely they thought, before we can see the occult meanings that lie deep down beneath their expressions of feeling, or the embodiments of their ideas. In all cases they seem to have thought with the heart, rather than with the brain. Their ideas came forth not cut, chiselled, and chilled by mere mental evolution; but rough and warm from the mould of the deep sympathy that lay between them and Nature and God. Nor is this emotionalism by any means foreign to the spirit of religion. Nay, rather it is its spirit and its form. The absence of natural affection is considered by St. Paul one of the distinguishing characteristics of paganism; and he who had earned that most illustrious of all titles, 'the beloved disciple,' and whose picture, by Albrecht Dürer at Nürnberg, is taken to be an exact portrait of Novalis, is also the apostle of love. There is

something in it after all, and cold intellectualism might
do well to study its effects and manifestations. How well
it would be for us all if we could believe in his own spirit
of splendid optimism, with Novalis, 'that love is the
final end of the world's history, the Amen of the Universe.'

SECTION III.

The great travelled

I have always to undergo a certain species of humiliation when I return home from the autumn holidays. People will ask, 'Where did you go this year?' And I have to answer, 'Only to Kilkee or Tramore!' Some gentle and modest questioner will say, 'I hope you enjoyed yourself and had good weather.' But there is a large, and ever-growing class, who, when they receive that reply, suddenly drop, or change the conversation, as if it were too painful to be pursued. You know them well. They are the world-explorers or globe-trotters, who have climbed the Pyramids and seen the Iceland geysers; who have glimpsed the interior of the Lamaseries of Thibet, and visited Siberian prisons; who have wondered (that is if they can wonder at anything) at the giant recumbent statue of Buddha in Ceylon, and read Aztec inscriptions in the ruined temples of Mexico; and to whom a dash at Constantinople or Cairo, or a run across the States to Vancouver, is considered a mere preliminary canter to a six months' holiday across the planet. They are formidable folk to meet; and modest people shrink away into a kind of coveted annihilation, until they get beyond the shadow of such experienced and ubiquitous neighbours.

Lesser experiences

There is a minor species of travelled people, however, who are more intolerant and – intolerable. They are the less enterprising but more impressive holiday-makers, who are modest enough to admit that they have only climbed Mont Blanc and seen the Passion-Play, but who always ask you, with a singular kind of pitiful contempt: 'Is it possible you have never seen Spain? Really now you ought to go to Spain!' And you feel very humble, and indeed half criminal; and you then and there resolve that your ultimate salvation depends on your having seen Spain, and that you must make the attempt, if it costs you your life. And you regard these experienced people with a kind of admiring wonder, and think how unhappily nature has dealth with you in not inspiring you with such glorious and profitable ambitions, and endowing you instead with a kind of hopeless inertia that makes the packing of a trunk or the purchase of a Cook's ticket a work to be dreaded and shunned. You admit how feebly you are equipped for life's serious work, and you make a desperate resolution that, come what will, you will see Spain and – no, or die!

Is travel a necessity?

On more sober reflection, however, and when the awful sense of your inferiority has vanished, you may be disposed to reflect, and reflecting, to ask yourself, Is travelling abroad really essential to existence? or to health and long life? or to education? And is it some innate or

66

congenital defect in your own nature that creates that re-
pugnance to going abroad for your holidays? For really,
it is just there that self-contempt comes in. And, as you
reflect, you probably will recall the case of the vast multitudes who never leave their own country, nay, their
own village, or townland; and whose lives are quite as
laborious as yours. Here are nuns, for instance, who for
fifty years have never gone outside these Convent walls;
who have seen the same little span of sky, the same little
patch of stars, during all that time; whose lives have been
lives of unremitting labour; and who now, in the evening
of life, take as cheerful an outlook over life and eternity
as the most philosophical, or rather eupeptic, optimist.
They listen to all recitals of foreign travel with a certain
amount of interest, but without much envy. They have
been content to live, to work, and are content to die. And
they have never known, even for a moment, that sen-
sation of ennui, which will attack people in the hotels
of Cairo, or the seraglios of Stamboul. Clearly then travelling abroad is not an essential of existence, or even
of health.

Nervous irritability

Then, again, there are three or four thousand people in
this remote parish, whose lives are draped in the same
sober monotone of place and scene and unintermittent
toil; and somehow they never think it a necessity of
existence to leave their homes, and see strange faces and
foreign climes. And they live, and have perfect health
and nerves and spirits, and thank God for His blessings,
nay even for His visitations, when He does come to

them under the disguise of a sorrow. Moreover, our fore-fathers and predecessors who had the same class of work to accomplish, with greater labour and more worries, never dreamed of an autumn holiday in France or Spain. And they lived to a ripe old age, and dropped peace-fully into peaceful graves. Ah, but we get depressed, and the springs of all mental and bodily activity get dulled or broken, and the doctor says: You must really go abroad, and see strange faces, and live under different circum-stances, and pick up fresh elasticity of spirits by change, change! Alas! it is the eternal question of nerves again. Nervous irritability is genius; nervous ennui, heresy; ner-vous literature, Ibsens and Maeterincks; and one and only one remedy, which is never more than a palliative, for the disease is deep-rooted; and that is change, change!

Travel and Education

But education? Is not travel here at least an essential? This too, may be doubted. How very few celebrities after all, made the 'grand tour'! Did Shakspere or Spenser cross the English Channel? Of those who did venture abroad in these days, how many repeated the exper-iment? Even in our times, let it be remembered that Byron and Shelley, Landor and Browning, were voluntary exiles, not travellers; and that if George Eliot could not get on without her annual trip to the continent, Tenny-son on the other hand rarely ventured from home. And Carlyle – ah! Carlyle, what it cost him to leave even his unhappy home at Chelsea, and get away amongst friends who were prepared to put pillows of roses under his nerve-distracted head! How he fumed and raged till he got back to his own dismal quarters again! And the two or three continental trips! 'Ach gott'! as he would say. Here is a specimen:

We got to Putbus, doing picturesquely the way. A beautiful Putbus indeed! where I had such a night as should be long memorable to me; big loud hotel, seabathing, lodgers with their noises, including plenteous coach-horses under my window, followed by noise of cats, brood-sows, and at 2 p.m. by the simultaneous explosion of two Cochin-China cocks, who continued to play henceforth, and left me what sleep you can fancy in such quarters... Adieu! Kiel Kissen! sloppy, greasy victual, all cold too, especially the coffee, and tea. Adieu! Deutschland! Adieu, travelling altogether, now and for ever more.

Lord Bacon

Really, this kind of thing reconciles you to your lot, if you are unable or unwilling to leave your own land. And if you have the least experience in travelling, and understand ever so little of its worries and annoyances, even in these days of luxury, you begin to think, that except for the extremely mercurial, who cannot sit still, and the extremely depressed, who require frequent changes, the game is hardly worth the candle. For, after all, in the whole of Europe this moment, how many things are there which you would really like to see? I do not say, how many places and things are there which you would like to be able to boast you saw. But how many things, persons, places, do you really covet with the eyes of your imagination? Lord Bacon gives you a handsome list for selection. He tells every traveller what he ought to see. Here is the list. 'The courts of princes, especially when they give audience to ambassadors; the courts of justice, while they sit and hear causes; Ecclesiastical Consistories; the churches and monasteries, with the monuments, which are therein extant; the walls and fortifications of cities and towns; havens and harbours, antiquities and ruins, libraries, colleges, disputations, and lectures; shipping and navies; houses and gardens of state and pleasure near great cities; armories, arsenals, magazines, exchanges, bourses, warehouses, exercises of horsemanship, fencing, soldiers and the like; comedies; treasures of jewels and robes; cabinets and rareties; and to conclude, whatever is memorable in the place where they go.'

What might interest

Of all these, about nine-tenths, I should say, are inaccessible to the ordinary traveller. Of these that are accessible, I confess the churches and monasteries alone would interest me; and one thing more, which the writer has omitted – the haunts and graves of great men. The room in the Roman college where St. Aloysius died would have more attraction for me than the Forum; and the places consecrated by the presence and ministrations of that sweet saint, Philip Neri, would drag me away from the spot where the mighty Cæsar fell. I would of course visit the Colosseum, but I would see only the mangled remains of the young Christian athletes and virgins whose limbs were rent asunder down there in its arena for the name of Christ. I would see it by moonlight also, but only to observe the shadowy figures who steal through the dark aisles and gather for sacred burial these hallowed remains. I would not give one precious quarter of an hour that I might spend in the sacred catacombs, to study the ruins of Pæstum, or trace the broken splendours of Hadrian's Villa; but I would rise with the dawn to be able to say Mass in that Mamertine prison, where the great Apostles were incarcerated, and where they baptised their gaolers with the waters of that miraculous spring that flows there in the dark beneath my feet.

A Dialogue

But education? We are wandering a little, as befits the subject. Travelling is essential to education? Perhaps so! But the most one can ever hope to extract from a travelled man is the exclamation: 'I saw that!' For example:

YOU. – 'The Parthenon which after so many thousand years is yet the noblest temple –'

TRAVELLER. – 'Oh yes! we saw the Parthenon, and the Acropolis!'

YOU. – 'It cannot be any longer maintained that Moorish or Saracenic influence was hostile to the arts of civilisation when that magnificent relic of their architecture, the Alhambra –'

TRAVELLER. – 'The Alhambra! Oh, we saw the Alhambra! 'Twas lovely!'

YOU. – 'And so if you want to see at their best Fountains' and Melrose –'

TRAVELLER. – 'Oh, yes! We were there. We saw both! They are exquisite.'

YOU. – 'I was just saying that if you want to see Fountains', or Melrose, visit them by moonlight. And you shall never know the vastness and sublimity of the Colosseum, until you startle the bats at midnight from its drapery of ivy, and –'

TRAVELLER. – 'Oh, yes! That's Byron, you know! No, Scott! Let me see:

> If you would see the – hem – aright
> Visit it by pale moonlight.

Isn't that it? No? Well then, 'twas Byron said:

> While stands the Colosseum, etc., etc.'

Who does not remember these poor little girls whom Ruskin has pilloried for ever in his *Fors Clavigera,* who read trashy novels, and eat sugared lemons all the way between Venice and Verona; and whose only remarks on the scenery and associations were: –
    'Don't these snow-caps make you cool?'
    'No – I wish they did.'
Are they types?

Recollection of Travels

Ah, but the memory of people, places, scenes, you have beheld! Isn't that worth preserving? Yes! I make the concession candidly. You have hit the bull's eye this time. The memory of travel is the real gain and blessing of travel, just as our memories of youth, and middle age, have a charm which our experiences did not possess. It is a curious fact and well worth investigating. Sitting here by the fireside, the eye of memory travels with an acute, and a certain kind of pathetic pleasure, over all the accidents and vicissitudes of our long journey. How little it makes of the worries and embarassments, how greatly it enhances the pleasures! You smile at the inconveniences of that long, dusty, tiresome railway journey, which you thought would never end; at the incivility of the porters or waiters, who contemptuously passed you by for greater folk; at the polite rudeness of the hotel keeper, who told you at twelve o'clock at night, when you stumbled half dazed from the railway carriage, that he had not a single room available; at the long avenue of waiters and waitresses who filed along the hotel corridor at your departure, expectant of much backsheesh, and ungrateful for little; at the cold Alpine heights, and the heat of Italian cities in the dogdays; at the little black-eyed beggar who served your Mass for a bajoccho, and turned somersaults at the altar free gratis; at the crush and the crowd, and the hustling and the elbowing in St. Peter's; at the awful extortions, made with the utmost politeness by these charming and intolerable natives; of the eternal peculation by the bland and smiling officials, etc., etc.

Scenes from memory

And you recall with a pleasure you never felt in the experience, the long, amber-coloured ranges of snow-clad mountains sweeping into sight as the train rushes through horrid gorges, or creeps slowly up some Alpine spur, that

73

slopes its declivities to meet the demands of science; the vast vistas of snow-white palaces above the ever-blue Mediterranean; the long day spent in the cool galleries face to face with immortal paintings; the twilight of great churches with all their half-veiled splendours of marble and pictures; that evening, when you watched the sun set across the Val d'Arno, and the strange blue twilight crept down before it, deepened into the purple-black of the night; the hour you spent above the graves of Shelley and Keats beneath the pyramid of Caius Cestius; that organ-recital in the great Italian cathedral, when you thought you saw the heavens opened and the angels ascending and descending; the shock and terror at the sudden rocking of the earth at Sorrento; the cool quadrangle in the Dominican convent, the play of the fountain, and the white-robed monks in the gallery overhead; the home-coming; the sight of ruddy English faces instead of the dusky, black-eyed Greek or Italian; the unpacking of your treasures; the steady settling down into the old groove of life, and the resumption of ancient habits.

Minor troubles

There is no doubt but that here is pleasure – deep unalloyed pleasure, independent of the vanity of being able to say: I was there! How do you account for it? Thus, my travelled friend. You see, wherever you went, you yourself were part and parcel of all you saw and felt; and you cast the shadow of self over all. And even a Lucretian philosopher will admit that self is the everpresent trouble, dimming and darkening all external splendours of space and time, and mingling its own bitter myrrh of thought and feeling with the brightest and most sparkling wine of life. Yes, you were worried here, and fretted there; the memory of your little annoyance was resh, and you took it with you; and here you were the victim of weariness and ennui, and you sang *Home, sweet Home!* in your heart. And your fellow-travellers, you remember, were sometimes disagreeable. You did not get on well together. It was all their fault, of course, they were so horribly impatient, and even ignorant. What pleased you displeased them. You would have wished to linger over that immortal canvas, which you knew you would never see again; or you would have liked to try your imperfect Italian on that laughing little nigger who rolled out his musical language as softly as he twisted the macaroni between his dirty fingers; but you were hurried on, on by your friends, and you found it hard to forgive them. They wanted to linger over dainty goods in shop-windows here and there, or to listen to some barrel-organ. You said very naturally: Can't they see and hear these things at home? Why do such people ever travel abroad?

Two classes

That too is simple of explanation. They have splendid physical health, and no minds worth speaking of. They cannot rest at home, just as the untamed animal spirits of a boy will not permit him to sit still for a moment. Now, Nature is a most even and impartial mother. She doles out her gifts with rigid impartiality. She has given some the affluence of great health and spirits, unburdened by imagination, and unstinted by reflection. To others (shall we say they are her favourites?) she gives the superior gifts of mentality, with all the divine gloom and depression that invariably accompany them. The former, mercurial in temperament, race across Europe, dip here and there in some antique fountain of art or literature, but instantly shake off the dreaded beads of too much thought; attend great ceremonies; enjoy the three hours' dinner at some palatial hotel; are noisy and communicative, and happy. They return fresh from their travels to tell their acquaintances: 'We have been there! Really now, you *must* go!' The others, if they can shake off the physical inertia which always accompanies and balances mental irritability, glide softly through Europe, linger over the spots sanctified by genius, spend quiet, dreamy hours in cool shady galleries, avoid the big hotels, watch Nature in the silence and the solitude of their hearts, and return to the winter fireside to embody in novel, or poem, their experiences, doubly hallowed in the light of memory. These are the men that make you despair, for they have the second sight, the vision that rises with the dawn, and haunts them till the dusk.

Memory and Art

This enchantment of the memory is really much the same as the enchantment of art. A beautiful picture gives you more pleasure than the beautiful reality it represents. You dare not say it is greater, or more perfect, or more true than Nature; but you feel greater pleasure in the contemplation of it than in the vision of the reality. Why? Because you are not a part of it. You see it from the outside. Your personality for ever jarring with itself and more or less out of tune, is not projected athwart it. You are something apart; and you see it as a something that has no connection whatsoever with you. Hence its peace, its calm, its truth, are soothing and restful. Or if there be figures in the pictures, or something dramatic and striking, for terror or for pathos, they do not touch you with any emotion, but that of curiosity and pleasure. You are in a theatre, and this is the stage; but the drama cannot touch you. That picture-frame, like that drop scene, cuts you away from the representation. You are a spectator, not an actor. But in real life, you cannot remain a spectator. Would to heaven you could! You will have touched the great secret of all human philosophy when you have brought to your mind, in its daily and hourly action, the conviction, that 'Life is a stage, and all men players and actors thereon.' But this is impossible and undesirable. You must play your own part, and it is mostly a tragic and solemn one.

The magic of childhood

This is the great secret of the happiness of childhood. Children are unconscious of themselves. They refer nothing to themselves. They hear of life, its vast issues, its tragedies, its trials, its weight of sorrows; but they can never for a moment believe that such things can affect themselves. The little things that do trouble them they pass lightly over, and forget. The little injustices that are done them they immediately condone. They have not as yet begun to refer all things in Heaven and Earth to themselves. They regard them as no part of their personality. Life is a picture – a pretty picture in a gilt frame. It is a gorgeous drama, where they can sit in the pit, or the boxes, according to their position in life, and look on calmly at Blue Beard and his wives, or the madness of Ophelia, or the smothering of Desdemona, while they crunch their caramels, or smear their faces with sugared fruit. Life is a pretty spectacle, created specially for their amusement. If any one were to say, There are Blue Beards yet in the world, and you may yet be a wife; or you may yet be an Ophelia, and carry around your bundles of rue; or, you may encounter your Iago, and have your handkerchief stolen; that child would laugh incredulously into your face. Unconsciousness and unbelief; or, rather, all-trusting faith in its immunity from sin and sorrow, are the glorious charters of childhood; as they are also symptoms of perfect, unbroken health.

All great work unconscious

The first moment of unrest, or subjectivity, or reference to ourselves, is the first moment also that marks our entrance on the stage of life; and it marks also the first step towards our failure. The unconscious actor is the greatest and the most perfect. Is it not a maxim of the stage; Lose your own personality in the person you represent? If you are introspective or self-examining, or curious to know what the audience is thinking of you, you will soon hear hisses and tumultuous condemnation. Just as in spiritual life, the secret not only of sanctity, but of happiness, is abandonment of self, and repose in God, so in our mere earthly life, we must abandon our selves to our inspirations or fail. The poet who tries to be a poet, will never be a poet. He may be an artist, or polisher, or filer of sentences and phrases; but he will always lack the higher afflatus. The saint, who thinks he is a saint, ceases to be a saint. The patriot, who begins to ask, how the welfare of his country will affect himself, ceases then and there to be a patriot. All great work is unconscious, and above all, unegotistical. The moment it becomes conscious, it becomes mechanical; and you can never turn a mechanic into a creator. Hence, when critics say that Tennyson was an artist before he became a poet, they imply that he never became a poet. For there never was a truer saying than the old trite one: Poëta nascitur. He may bury his gifts, and stifle his creative powers, and become a *Poëtes apoietes;* but his is a birth-right that can never be bought or sold.

The Unrevealed

There is another great advantage in this reserve of foreign travel. Something as yet remains unrevealed. Remember that ennui is the disease of modern life; and that ennui is simply the repletion of those who have tasted too speedily, or too freely, at the banquet of life. Unhappy is the man who has parted with all his illusions; and such is he in a most special manner, who has seen all things, and tried all, and found all wanting. For, the first view, the first experience, is the poetry of existence. And poetry, like reverence, will not tolerate familiarity. You won't rave about Alps, or Apennines, the second time you see them. You have acquired knowledge, and lost a dream. Now, the dream for ever remains with one, who has not seen, but believed. The mystery, the wonder, the charm, are yet before him. He may yet see and be glad. Earth and sea hold all their miracles in reserve for him. He cannot sit down in middle age, and say: 'I have seen all things beneath the sun; and lo! all is vanity!' No! he will not say that, as long as the bright succession of the world's wonders may yet file before him. He has always a reserve; and sinks even into his grave with all the hope and fascination, all the glamour and straining eyes of inexperience.

The pleasure of novelty

To one living at a distance from railways the whistle of the engine gives a thrill of novelty, and a sudden pleasure. There is a romance, and even a poetry, in railways. At least, to one unaccustomed to leave home, a railway journey is a rare enjoyment. He cannot see the great, smooth engine rolling into the platform, or behold the faces at the windows, or take his seat, without a certain excitement, or nervous thrill, that is utterly unknown to the experienced traveller. The comfortable cushioned seat, the electric light overhead, the mirrors all around him, the new, strange faces, each with its secret soul looking out, anxious, hopeful, or perplexed; the very isolation of his travelling companions and the mystery that

hangs around their unknownness; the quiet that settles
down on the carriage as it glides out so smoothly from
the station; the rapid succession of scenes that move
across the field of vision – all is novel, all is unexperienced, all delightful! He would give the world to know
who, or what, is that old gentleman, who has pulled his
rug around him and is buried in his papers; or that
young, pale fellow, who is so much at home, he must be a
much-travelled man; or that young girl, who is gazing so
steadfastly through the window. And the real pleasure is,
that all is mystery, and wonder, and the unknown, even
to the end.

A Cunarder

Twenty-five years ago I thought that a Cunard, or a
White Star Liner, outward bound, was the most interesting sight on earth. I think so still. The silence of its
movements, its obedience to the slightest touch, the risks
and hazards before it, when it is but a speck on the illimitable deep, and the moonlight is all around it, or when
it is rocked from billow to billow, like a cork; but above
all, the strange, mysterious faces that look from behind
their veils at you, and the strange history behind the veils,
and the strange drama that is being enacted there – all
conspire to make that floating caravanserai one of those
objects of interest and wonder that carry with them always the glamour and mystery of another world. That is
to the inexperienced. I dare say that commercial traveller
who has crossed the Atlantic twenty times, and who
seems so much at home there upon the sloping deck

thinks otherwise. Probably he is calculating how much he will win at poker or euchre; or what seat he shall have at table. That lady, too, who has just done Europe, and who looks so tired and *blasée*, is just hoping that the beastly voyage may be soon over, that she may plunge once more into the glorious whirl of New York excitement. But to the untravelled, the inexperienced, all is wonder and mystery, from the invisible being up aloft who is the master of our destinies, to the grimy fireman, who comes up from the Inferno, to catch one breath of fresh, salt air.

Incognito

If the untravelled is wise he will speak to no one, but in monosyllables, and preserve his own incognito and in-experience to the end. Thus, he, too, will be a mystery, and somewhat interesting to others, who will be dying to penetrate behind his mask. And all around will bear the glamour of unknownness to his imagination. It is horrible – that disillusion about people, around whom you have woven your own webs of fancy. Now, if you accost that commercial traveller, you will – you must reveal the fact that you are crossing the Atlantic for the first time; and down you go several degrees in his esteem. Or, if you are happy enough to get acquainted with that young lady in the canvas chair, blue-veiled, and with infinite rugs about her, she will probably tell you, 'She has just done Yurrup, and is tired of the whole show.' And the airy web of fancy is rudely torn asunder. Or, if you should come to know the officers, and they with their usual kindness, tell you about their vessel, and their experiences; or gossip about the passengers, or show you the tremendous mechanism that is the heart-throb and life-pulse of the ship, you will have come down to the stand-point of commonplace; and before you step ashore at New York, your nerves will have cooled down, and you will regard the ship of fancy as a black old hulk, with a hideous brass kettle in the centre.

Reticence and Reverence

There is a great deal more than we are accustomed to think in this habit of reticence and reverence. Touch not, taste not, if you would keep fresh the divine fancies that spring from a pure imagination, excited by pure and inspiring literature. It was the irreverent curiosity of our first parents that opened their eyes to unutterable things. They touched, tasted, and saw. Better for them and their posterity had they kept the reverence due to the behests of the Most High, and with it their unsullied innocence and blessed want of knowledge. There was a tradition of our childhood that the mother bird would desert a nest once breathed upon by others. The place was profaned, and she would haunt it no longer, even though the blue or speckled eggs would never come to maturity. Even so with the spirit. It refuses to go back to places once dishallowed by knowledge. It prefers to hover over lonely heights, and to haunt unpeopled solitudes; and there to keep the virginal freshness of its inexperience unsullied by knowledge that opens the eyes of mind and body, but blinds the vision of the soul.

But, coming back under the umbrage and gloom of great trees from the illimitable expanse of sea and sky, I ask myself why I experience a sudden narrowing and contraction of spirit, although my mind is as free and untrammelled as before. And why do people, sick of their prison houses and the narrow limitations of daily life, seek for freshness down there as close to the sea as they can go? For they will not look at the sea from afar, nor from safe vantage grounds, but they creep down and sit on rocks that overhang the tremendous depths; and imperil their lives by going lower and lower still, until their feet are washed by the incoming, irresistible tides. What do they want? What do they seek? It is not pure air alone. That they can have on mountain summits. Yet they never go to the mountains. But the most unpoetic, unromantic, prosaic people will seek the sea-shore; and remain there the whole day long, and tear themselves away from it with difficulty; and even when it is only a memory and a dream, will speak of it the whole winter long, and bear the worries and work of the year in the hope that they shall seek and see the sands and waves and the far horizon again.

Alpine prisons

I experienced a similar sense of imprisonment and freedom once in a very brief holiday abroad. I never saw the Alps from their summits; and, therefore must not speak disparagingly of them. But I passed through gorges and ravines, and lonely valleys, several thousands of feet above the sea, but everywhere felt, even on the highest altitudes, as if I where walking the flagged courtyard of a prison, with impassable, unscaleable granite walls around and above, grinding and crushing the spirit. Perhaps if I had stood on the St. Bernard or Monte Rosa, and looked around on the white cold crests that capped the undulations of crags and peaks without number my sensations would have been different. But I well remember drawing a great breath of relief, when the train steamed out from beyond Interlaken, and we passed by Fribourg, and saw in a moment the Lake Leman, unbounded in that direction but by the sky. It was just as if a person, half-asphyxiated by the thick air of a prison cell, had been suddenly summoned to life, liberty, and pure, sweet wholesome breathing again.

The Unbounded

I cannot explain it, except by the theory of our universal, insatiable craving after the Unbounded, the Infinite. You imprison the soul when you limit its aspirations. It must be in touch with the Universe. It is the one thing on earth, the only thing, that cannot make its home here. All things else are content to do their little work, perform their little part, and die. Winds arise and blow, and pass away; seas come and go, and scatter themselves on the sands; leaves bud, and develop, and fall; animals are born, pass on to maturity, and return to the inorganic state. Man alone looks out and beyond this planet. Here he hath no lasting dwelling-place. His soul is with the stars. And there-

fore it chafes at its imprisonment in the body; and even
the accidental environments of place and scenery affect
this strange homeless exile that is for ever pining after
its own country. How sweetly the Church interprets this
feeling in the beautiful Benediction hymn:

> *Qui vitam sine termino*
> *Nobis donet in patria.*

And this is the vision we look for when we strain our
eyes across the sunlit sea; and dream of things beyond
the visible horizon, but not beyond the horizon of our
hopes.

Denial of Destiny

Hence the secret of the *Welt-Schmerz*, the dreary hopeless pessimism that has sunk like a thunder cloud on the
minds of all modern thinkers, and blackens every page
of modern literature, is that these unhappy unbelievers
deny their destiny and vocation, and denying it, refuse to
pursue it, and sink down into mere denizens of earth. The
moment they yield to the sordid temptation of disbe-
lieving their own immortality, they excommunicate themselves from the Universe. They are no longer part of the
great, stupendous whole. Life becomes a wretched span,
limited on both sides by the gulf of nothingness, instead
of being the prelude to the vast eternity of existence that
is connoted by immortality. Man is a clod, a senseless
atom, an inorganic substance, galvanized for a moment
into an organism. He is but a self-conscious, yet insignifi-
cant part of the chemistry of Nature, with no relations,

least of all eternal correspondence, with the vast spirits of the Universe.

Mad King Lear

I cannot help thinking that mad Lear upon the moorlands, whipped by the storm, disowned by his daughters, and accompanied by a fool, is the type of such unhappy beings. For irreligion is insanity. Just as the latter is but the partial and distorted view of the diseased mind that looks out at Nature; so the former is the half-vision that refuses to see the perfect whole, rounded into unity and uniformity under the Almighty Hand. And forth the discrowned victim goes, 'the king walking in the mire' as the wise man saw him, the storms of life and tempestuous throught are around him, the children of his genius execrate him for his alienation of their birthright, he has with him as 'guide, philosopher, friend,' a fool, – shall we say, his own darkened and stammering intellect? And the gloom and desolation grow deeper and deeper around him, for he sees no hope or prospect of the dawn; but only the night, and the night, and the night!

The luxury of Melancholy

It is true there is a certain strange luxury in this intellectual melancholy and depression. But the motive is not sane; the experience is not wholesome. However much we may pity the loneliness, or admire the genius, of all

87

these modern pessimists, 'and their name is legion,' they are undoubtedly a wretched and degenerate lot. Sadness is their portion; life has a dreary outlook to them; the heat of battle is not in their veins; the cry of victory is not on their lips. Life is all a hideous drama, until death tears down the curtain, and the lights are extinguished; and with tears on their pallid faces, the spectators pass out into the night. How that dreary, dull undertone of sadness rolls through all modern literature! Never a note of triumph, never a psalm of hope, never a glorious prophetic pæan about the future that is to be, where man shall touch his real spiritual evolution, and reach his finality amongst his brethren of the skies. But a low deep wail, musical enough, if you like, echoing along the minor chords of human misery, and sobbing itself away into silence, unless the wind moaning among the tangled grasses and nettles above the deserted and forgotten graves, can be taken as the echo in Nature of the threnodies that wailed from such desolate and despairing lives.

A Procrustean bed

'Our desires went beyond our destinies,' they say, 'and therefore we are unhappy.' Nay, it was not your desires, but your powers, that reached beyond your imagined and narrowed destinies, and hence you were unhappy. You would not recognise facts. You stretched yourselves on a Procrustean bed, and sought a comfort that would not come. You were made other than you thought. You disputed the very laws of Nature when you contended that those faculties of reason, imagination, affection,

88

were limited in their development and enjoyment to the transient objects of the senses and of this lower life. You refused to believe in the infallible proportion of things; the rigid, inexorable law that destiny must proportion itself to Nature; and that the eternal harmonies that govern all things demanded an infinity for cravings that were infinite; an eternity for love that was stronger than death. But this you refused to accept. You made yourselves monsters, anomalies in creation. Like the barbarians of old, you proved to yourselves that the destiny of the sun was to sink in the sea, and be extinguished. You could not understand how to-morrow, he is destined to rise, and 'exult again like a giant, to run his destined course.'

Rêveurs

And hence we have, especially in France, all these *rêveurs,* and *penseurs,* and moralists, and soliloquists, fleeing from practical life, and with heads bent and drooping eyes, wandering through the solitudes of Nature, and talking to trees, and trying to catch in the murmur of the stream, or the whisper of the wind, some answer to the eternal questionings of weary and disspirited minds. The rush from society to Nature is a curious phenomenon of our age. It is a symptom of the strange morbidity that has come down upon the world, since philosophers and poets first disturbed, then broke up, the healthy equilibrium of Christian teaching in the minds of their disciples. The return to Nature, the elimination of its omnipresent, beneficent Creator, the searching everywhere for the great god, Pan, the disappointment, the unrest, the self-disgust and weariness, are visible everywhere in those pages that interpret emotions and thoughts, which probably the eyes of men would never have seen, if all this solitariness and introspection and reverie were not tinged with that species of affectation and vanity, which is at once the cause and effect of all that eccentricity, which drives men from the orbit of their species, and compels them to an existence, unhappy and alone.

The Eternal Child

How different the eternal hope, the far visioning the ever exultant pæan that rises from the Christian heart! It is always childhood and morning, and great peace, and eternal, invincible faith in the ultimate perfection of all feeble an unstable things. Nature, the sombre and veiled companion of the children of unfaith, becomes the revealed and laughing nurse of the children of belief. She, too, is but the beloved servant in our Father's home where we are the children. She puts on no Sybilline airs, utters no phrenetic prophecies, conceals no subtle meanings, speaks no mysterious language. All the occult mysticism that unbelief affects to see beneath her phenomena, resolves itself into the sweet simplicities of one, who is a handmaiden to the great Lord of all things. And hence, we are not frightened by her power, nor terrified by her magic, nor awed by her sublimity. All her motions and signs we refer to a cause and an end. We appreciate their beauty and holiness; but rest not there. All things

in her and about her round to perfection – that final
perfection which is God!

The decline of the year

From summer maturity and splendour, the year is moving
steadily onward to the decline and ashen greyness of
winter again. The garden beds, shorn of all their blossoms through the slips that are to be reserved for next
summer, look mutilated of all their refined strength and
beauty, their strong stalks having developed into wood,
the special horror of a gardener. There is a smell of frost
in the early evening, as the fogs rise ghostlike from the
valleys; and the sun has sunk down from the imperial
heights of summer and taken humbly a lower arc in the
heavens. How swiftly has the summer gone! It seems but
yesterday that so late as nine or half-past nine o'clock, I
watched the trees blackening against the saffron sunset.
Now, it is pitch dark at eight o'clock. The swallows are
training their young for the autumnal flight; and holding
more frequent conclaves in the skies and on the roofs.
The hum of the threshing machine comes mournfully
from afar off. I see the rich produce of the harvest flung
into its gaping mouth to come forth reed and grain. The
stags are belling in yonder forest. The first patch of gold
is seen on the chestnut. Nature is winding up her little
affairs in view of her approaching demise. And the winds
are beginning to rise, and practise their winter requiems
over a dead and silent world.

The great Transatlantic liners are filled, every berth, with 'travelled men from foreign lands,' rushing homewards to the little roof that shelters them and the little lives which are linked with theirs. The equinoctial gales are blowing in their teeth; yet they speed onwards. Home and love await them across the white breakers of the angry seas. Everywhere the turbulent riotousness of summer is giving way to the rigid order of winter. The hatches are being fastened down; and everything must be snug and tight before the rain, and the snow, and the storm. The time is coming for the merry fire, and the beloved book, and the tea-urn, and the curtained and carpeted luxuries of home. And outside, housed too, forevermore against all the dangers and vicissitudes of life, the beautiful, mysterious dead sleep on in their silent cities. The moon-light throws black shadows of shrub or cross athwart their graves. The seasons come and go; and they are swept round and round in the swift diurnal march of Mother Earth. But they are at rest. Theirs is the peace of eternity. Theirs the fruition. Ours still the faith and the hope, – in God, in His eternal laws, in our own souls.

> I trust in Nature, for the stable laws
> Of beauty and utility – Spring shall plant,
> And Autumn garner to the end of time.
> I trust in God, – the right shall be the right,
> And other than the wrong, whilst He endures.
> I trust in my own soul, that can perceive
> The outward and the inward, – Nature's good
> And God's.

THE SADNESS OF AUTUMN
by Canon Sheehan

Although he is famous and beloved as a novelist, Canon Sheehan was also one of the most farseeing and penetrating thinkers of the second half of the nineteenth century – the period in which were forged, painfully and laboriously, the ideals that were to culminate in the Rising of 1916.

Here we meet him as commentator and philosopher, finding sermons in stones and good in everything. He tells us of his interests: Plato and Aristotle; the Greek Fathers; Wordsworth; Frankenstein's Monster – all fascinate him equally. But there is nothing coldly intellectual in his approach; the one unifying thread running through this wide variety of topics is the author's concern for human beings. He describes a great storm that raged around his presbytery at Doneraile, bringing into play the eloquence the readers of his novels will expect. The sound of the wind was 'like the cry of the angels who abandoned Jerusalem to its fate'. The night before the storm, a tramp had wandered into the Canon's garden. His housekeeper had announced this visitor as a 'gentleman' – as Canon Sheehan wryly observes, we are so polite in Ireland that everyone is a 'gentleman' who doesn't actually sport a title. He goes on to tell us why he likes tramps. 'Tramps, comets, variable stars... flotsam and jetsam of heaven and earth – I have a curious sympathy with them all.' This particular tramp lies, shamelessly exploits the charity he is offered, instantly transmutes the money he is given into whiskey – and yet Canon Sheehan writes of him with humour and delight.

He writes with equal affection of a friendly robin who hops into his garden. With a deep brown back and a scarlet brest-plate and 'round wondering eyes watching mine'. Then the Canon realises that the robin is really watching a fine fat worm; the robin bites him into halves and then into quarters: 'He was his own butcher.' So much for sentiment...

The Sadness of Autumn is indeed never sentimental, for it is written out of the love of truth and the love of God.

85342 329 6   60p

THE LONELINESS OF WINTER
by Canon Sheehan

The best-loved of all Irish novelists, it is sometimes forgotten that Canon Sheehan was also a critic, a commentator, and a philosopher, concerned with all the great issues that still obsess men as deeply as they did in the nineteenth century when he wrote his books.

Here he confronts his material directly, discarding the mask of the novelist. He discusses the Psalms; Cardinal Newman; compares De Quincey with Richter and Saint Augustine with Maine de Biran; surprises us with Thomas Carlyle's views on the Mass; reminds us of the vision of Boethius; and, perhaps most significantly of all, finds inspiration in the pensees of Pascal. He writes of the great philosophers Kant and Fichte – not, to our surprise and delight, in abstract terms, but telling the all too human story of Kant's refusal to help Fichte return to his native province.

Both the novelist's sense of drama and the priest's compassion are implicit in his account of a hospital he visited. He reminds us how fortunate we are to be in good health – even to be alive. For a tormented moment he evokes a world of pain and decay – 'that little nodule of flesh is incipient cancer, that flush and chill is typhus, that sudden pain in your left arm is cardiac trouble –' and we remember how thin was the crust that divided the comfortable surface of Victorian life from the threat of disease and death.

But soon he has put gloom behind him and he is writing in a mood of perfect serenity of 'this great red moon, burning through the latticed trees and then paling away as it mounted higher and higher in heaven, was a symbol of the perfect beauty to which all things tend...' His love of nature and his poetic sense of its beauties never fail him. *The Loneliness of Winter* reflects that love; it reflects also Canon Sheehan's understanding of man and of his total dependence on the love of God.

85342 330 x

60p

THE MAGIC OF SPRING
by Canon Sheehan

Canon Sheehan's unique fame as the best-loved of Irish storytellers has obscured the fact that he was a thinker and social critic as well as a creative artist. In fact, he was the forerunner of the modern Catholic novelists: as concerned as they are with man facing a spiritual and intellectual crisis that may change in externals but remains the same in essence.

Here, in a book that combines the quiet mood of the essayist with the insight of the novelist, Canon Sheehan finds some virtue and considerable fascination in everything he discusses. His range is immense: Cato and Dante; the characters of Dickens; the morality of Goethe; Stevenson and Robert Browning – these are only a few of his topics. He tells again the story of the pathetic meeting between the philosopher Bishop Berkeley and the Oratorian Malebranche in Paris; and one can sense his novelist's romantic feeling for disorder when he discusses the canonisation of Saint Benedict Joseph Labre in 1883. Canon Sheehan exults in the paradox of 'this beggar, this tramp with just enough rags to cover him but not to protect him, raised on the alters of the Church for the veneration of the faithful!' He describes how the saint rejoiced that men shrank from him and loathed him; how he sought humiliation 'as fools seek honours'.

The novelist's imagination comes to the fore in his description of a fire: a vivid account of the burning of a great mill, a conflagration so vast that 'the clouds overhead were reddened as in a winter sunset, when the light falls lurid and glaring. The shadows were deep and black; a strange colour tinted hyacinth, tulip, and daffodil in the same monastic and uniform tint.'

The Magic of Spring is a work of great variety, coloured by Canon Sheehan's keen perception of nature, his love of man, and his awareness of God.

85342 327 x   60p

First published in the Netherlands.
Made and printed in Holland by Van Boekhoven-Bosch nv, Utrecht